THIRTEEN LESSONS THAT SAVED
THIRTEEN LIVES

THIRTEEN LESSONS THAT SAVED
THIRTEEN LIVES

THE THAI CAVE RESCUE

JOHN VOLANTHEN
With Matt Allen

Aurum

First published in hardback in 2021 by Aurum
an imprint of The Quarto Group.

The Old Brewery, 6 Blundell Street,
London, N7 9BH, United Kingdom.
www.QuartoKnows.com/Aurum

A catalogue record for this book is available from the British Library.

ISBN: 978-0-7112-6609-4

E-book ISBN: 978-0-7112-6611-7

1 2 3 4 5 6 7 8 9 10

Cover design by Luke Bird
Typeset in Adobe Caslon Pro by SX Composing DTP, Rayleigh, Essex, SS6 7EF
Printed and bound by CPI Group (UK) Ltd, Croydon, CR0 4YY

CONTENTS

Introduction   7

Lesson 1: Start with *Why Not?*   23

Lesson 2: Listen to the Quiet Voice   43

Lesson 3: Zoom In, Zoom Out   63

Lesson 4: Rest and Decompress   81

Lesson 5: One Breath at a Time   101

Lesson 6: Expect the Unexpected   121

Lesson 7: Step Up and Step Back   139

Lesson 8: Harnessing Teamwork and Trust   155

Lesson 9: Hurry Up and Do . . . *Nothing*   173

Lesson 10: Keep it Simple   193

Lesson 11: Rehearse. Then Repeat   217

Lesson 12: Make Success a Habit   237

Lesson 13: Define Your Own Happiness   261

End Note: Full Circle   279

The Thirteen Lessons   281

Acknowledgements   285

Glossary   287

John Volanthen   292

Index   293

INTRODUCTION

They were alive.

I counted all thirteen faces with my flashlight as they peered back through the gloom. *One: Titan. Two: Mix. Three: Dom. Four: Pong.* Stuck inside a cave for nearly two weeks, unsurprisingly they looked tired and frightened. *Five: Mark. Six: Tern. Seven: Biw. Eight: Adul. Nine: Note. Ten: Nick.* T-shirts hung from their malnourished bodies as they shuffled towards us like ghouls: waving, pointing, almost disbelieving that anyone could have emerged from the chilly underground floodwaters that had trapped them for the best part of a fortnight. *Eleven: Tee. Twelve: Night. And finally, number thirteen, the Wild Boars football team coach, Ek.* This was a group of boys the world had already written off as dead. The football team stuck on a small bank in the belly of Tham Luang, a sidewinding labyrinth of caves positioned underneath the Doi Nang Non mountain range on the border between Thailand and Myanmar, and impenetrable to any rescue attempts – *until now.*

Some of the kids shouted out.

'Thank you,' yelled a voice at the back.

'Are we going out today?' said another, waving into the inky darkness.

The smallest boy in the group slumped to the ground and sobbed silently. The poor kid looked distraught, which came as no great surprise given it was 2 July 2018 and the kids, aged between eleven and seventeen, plus twenty-five-year-old Ek, had first been reported missing on 23 June 2018. According to news reports, the date had been important. Night was celebrating his seventeenth birthday and the plan had been for an hour-long group excursion into the cave. For the Wild Boars, this was a big deal. Night had been the first of the team to reach such a milestone age; he was the oldest member in the group and the other boys looked up to him. Meanwhile, Ek, the responsible adult, had come along to guide everybody through the tunnels. The feeling was that all the boys within the team would be in safe hands.

The chances are, had anyone known that the previous day's heavy storms were still filling the caves with floodwater, they would have warned the Wild Boars off such an excursion. Under those circumstances, crawling inside was incredibly risky because cave systems like Tham Luang held an unnerving reputation. On a bad day they could flood quickly, and with lethal results. What might have seemed like a fairly innocuous team adventure into the dark on a grey, but hot afternoon, a cool way to hang out after football training, very quickly twisted into a nightmarish ordeal as waves of churning water surged through the tunnels at high speed, transforming a series of interlinking caverns into watery tombs. Escaping on foot was suddenly unimaginable.

Claustrophobic, narrow cracks in the rock, and passages that had seemed like a tight squeeze on the way in had become sunken death traps. Every escape route was impossible to negotiate without underwater breathing apparatus, serious experience and a steady nerve, so there was certainly no way out for a bunch of kids with zero knowledge of cave diving. Climbing to higher ground inside the cavern in search of safety, the waters around them still rising, the Wild Boars had huddled together for warmth instead. Prayer was all they had left. The team would need rescuing, that's if anybody knew they'd entered the cave at all.

But they did. After twenty-four hours, the story of their disappearance started to creep across news feeds all over the world. Very soon, TV crews and journalists were flying to Thailand. Online, people were issuing their hopes, prayers and platitudes. And it was because of the news that I had decided to offer my services, having eventually figured out that given our experience and expertise in such high-pressure situations, my regular diving partner Rick Stanton and I were best placed to conduct a search and rescue mission. All my cave rescues had been unpaid. Rather than a career, I had always considered these operations as my contribution to what was a small community of divers. For work I ran my own IT business. In Thailand I was a volunteer.

But commitments of this kind had certainly led me on an interesting journey. I'd been a cave diver for thirty-odd years, and alongside Rick I had set two records*. The first was for diving 76 metres into Wookey Hole, Somerset in 2004 – the greatest depth recorded in a British cave. I then broke the record for the longest exploration into a cave when, as a team we dived 8,800 metres into the Pozo Azul caverns in Spain's Rudrón Valley in 2010. Rick and I worked together regularly. We first dived as part of a team in Gough's Cave, Somerset, during 2002, where I'd carried in a series of diving cylinders for weeks to help explore the end of the cave. In a single dive, Rick was able not

---

* UK cave divers will usually explore alone. Sometimes they deliberately put distance between themselves and any other divers underwater. This might seem counter-intuitive, but in small passages with low visibility, a buddy or partner can often be a hindrance to solving problems.

only to visit, but to extend the end of the tunnels and I realised that he'd built his own rebreather* to do so. I decided that constructing one of my own was a vital next step; the alternative was to hang up my fins. I chose the former, and a strong partnership developed between the two of us.

Together, Rick and I had previously conducted a number of high-profile rescue operations, as well as volunteering to work in body recovery missions, a grizzly business, and as a result I had developed the skill set, confidence and knowhow to execute the job. But having arrived in Thailand and negotiated the political machinations surrounding what should have been a fairly straightforward humanitarian effort, and having spent several days attempting to find the stricken team, I had come to fear the worst. During dives I had to wriggle against murky, churning currents and through body-hugging cracks in the rock, my head torch unable to pierce the murky water. Tham Luang felt impenetrable.

'There's no chance those kids have survived,' I thought after one particularly gruelling dive. '*Is there?*'

One night I even went so far as to mentally prepare myself for a hellish, endgame event. I visualised swimming into a tunnel choked with what looked like discarded plastic bags, ragged clothing and shoes, only to realise it was an underwater morgue. Mentally, the process, though morbid, steeled me for the grimmest of outcomes, but I wasn't the only one preparing for such a negative event. The Thai authorities had all but given up hope, too, and the mood within the divers I'd been working alongside was just as doom-laden – a group that included my diving partner

---

* A device that recycles the diver's exhaled breath, removing carbon dioxide and adding oxygen. It is very much more efficient than open-circuit regulators at depth.

Rick, Belgian cave diver Ben Reymenants, plus units from the Thai Navy SEALs, some members of the US military and a handful of Australian police divers. It was a widely shared view among us all that once the waters had retreated from Tham Luang, some of the group would be faced with the unenviable task of fishing a number of corpses from the muddy pools.

But we'd been wrong. *Those kids had made it.*

In the end, when Rick and I had located the Wild Boars' whereabouts, it had an unlikely feel to it. On 30 June, word filtered through to the rescue teams that our efforts had gone as far as they could, and so a colleague took us on a day trip around the mountain, even as the storm was still raging about us. I was quite happy for the distraction: we had been trapped by circumstance and bureaucracy, and the Thai government, keen not to create a PR disaster, wanted to hold all the foreign volunteer teams on site. Their fear was that a photo of the rescuers might be taken as they packed away equipment and tidied up their kit. That image would send an international message that thirteen lives had been lost and the authorities had been powerless to help.

Then everything changed. The weather calmed a little and the rapids that had once held us back from pushing deeper in to the Tham Luang tunnels began a slow retreat. We decided to make one more attempt at finding the Wild Boars. Supported by the American and Thai rescue teams in attendance, we spent two days swimming further into the caverns and fixing guidelines – the kind of rope you might see used on a mountain expedition as a team of high-altitude climbers attack the summit of some inaccessible peak. Underwater in a cave, however, these ropes worked in two ways. The first was to serve as a route marker in the churning, sediment-heavy waters. The second was as a tool for forward momentum: by pulling on the line, a following diver could move more easily past stalactites and stalagmites, through rocky, body-hugging tubes and into vast pools with no immediate escape routes. If you haven't guessed already, cave rescues are no task for the faint-hearted.

As the search progressed and the floodwaters retreated, little by little, Rick and I realised that we were suddenly able to penetrate much further into the cave than any previous dive had managed so far. The bad news was that time was against us. We had been working through the cave for five hours. Our air supply was fading, and I knew we needed to turn around if we were to make it back to the cave entrance safely. As the famous mountain climber, Ed Viesturs had once claimed, 'Getting to the top of Everest is optional. Getting down is mandatory.' A similar theory applies to cave diving.

Let me explain. Once a diver has hit a certain level in his air tanks, even with rebreathing equipment – the air mask and tank that recycles used air to create a near constant supply – they then have to commit to making the journey home. (The golden rule is to think in thirds: one-third of a tank for the way in; one-third for the way out; one-third for emergencies.) Having pushed past what were my normal and acceptable safety margins, while laying out nearly all the guideline as we moved deeper into Tham Luang, I'd reached my turning point. The water was getting cold and the grim visualisation exercise I'd undertaken a few days earlier seemed set to transform into a horrific reality. While moving through a dark sump*, my vision distorted by rushing

---

* A flooded section of cave passage where the water reaches the roof.

water and churning mud, I bumped into a heavy object moving in the current. Then something brushed against my legs.

'Oh, God,' I thought. 'Have I just found the first body?'

I kicked forward into the murk and spotted what I thought was a skeletal limb floating towards me. It bobbed and swayed in the currents. *Was I going to find a torso, a head, and a pair of legs as well?* My stomach tensed. I reached forward to make a grab for it, my breath slowing as the lifeless shape in the gloom turned out to be nothing more than a discarded length of rubber piping. Not that I felt any less concerned. As ominous signs nudged me in the currents, an unpleasant discovery seemed inevitable.

With each passing minute, my desire to turn back only mounted further. I even prayed that the rope I had been feeding into the caves might run out – because we would have to return to the safety of the entrance once the last of our guidelines had been set. But then the passage roof seemed to rise up. We had emerged into another large air pocket and I immediately took in our surroundings. We were in a dark cavern and the scene around me seemed so different to the murky underworld we'd been moving through a second or two earlier.

The cave was large and only half-filled with water. There was no light, apart from the beam of my head torch, but I felt a sensory jolt; a weird signal that everything around us was *different*. More than anything, there was an immediate, instinctive feeling that an unusual happening was in motion. At first it was intangible. There was a flicker in my peripheral vision. I sensed movement nearby. *Was someone watching us?* Then I noticed Rick. He'd taken off his face mask. As his head turned this way and that, I noticed his nostrils flaring. *He was sniffing the air.*

'Take a smell,' he said, pointing to the cavern's dark corners. 'Tell me what you get . . .'

The stink, when I inhaled deeply, was heavy, ripe and strong enough to twist the stomach. 'Oh no, Rick. That's rotting flesh.'

He nodded sombrely. We had finally discovered what we'd assumed would be a graveyard.

Except, we hadn't.

There was a sound behind me, then another. As I twisted around it was hard to take in the reality of what was happening. A group of boys had gathered silently at the water's edge and were pointing. *It was the Wild Boars*! It had to be . . . *But, how?* With barely any food between them, or a proper source of drinking water, it seemed unthinkable that they could have survived for ten days. Certainly, very few people in the rescue team had fancied their chances – and yet, here they were. I couldn't believe they had made it through the flood.

Instinctively, I shouted across to them. 'How many of you?'

There was no response, but I could hear Rick counting. 'One, two, three . . .'

Moving closer to the bank, I shone my head torch towards the faces looking back at me.

'Eleven, twelve, thirteen . . . *They're all here.*'

Brilliant.

But the situation had unsettled me a little and, at first, I felt overwhelmed by the enormity of what to do next. I had no idea of how we were going to transport the team back to safety in what would be a gruelling swim of around four hours, with the current behind us. Then, I mentally broke the situation down into manageable phases. Assessing the health and wellbeing of the stranded team had to be the first priority. Apart from Ek, the coach, the Wild Boars were kids; they were starved, which meant they would be close to their physical and emotional breaking points, though given the different ages within the group, some would undoubtedly be tougher than others. I knew that Rick had a Snickers bar shoved into his wetsuit pocket, but dishing it out at that point would have only created a *Lord of the Flies*-style conflict, in which the strongest boys feasted on small bites of chocolate while the weakest starved.

Reading the room, and guessing the implications of handing out the measliest of food parcels, Rick pushed the chocolate bar further into his suit. From now on, paying close attention to the tiniest details would be key, but building morale was just as important. As a volunteer with the Somerset Cub Scouts, I had gathered a fair level of experience in working alongside kids in challenging, outdoor environments: I often took groups caving where there was the possibility that somebody might lose their nerve, or experience a minor meltdown while exploring what could be a fairly intimidating environment. To succeed in Tham Luang I would need to apply similar levels of empathy, plus a good bedside manner as the situation unfolded around me. *I would pretend the Wild Boars were Cub Scouts.* In which case, it was important to reassure them by presenting confidence and authority.

'We are coming,' I said, hoping to pass on the idea that their survival wasn't entirely dependent on the actions of two middle-aged blokes from England. 'Many people are coming. Believe . . .'

I said it again, to make absolutely sure they understood. *'Believe.'*

Every action and gesture was being captured on a headcam given to us by the Thai Navy SEALs, and during the rescue's aftermath, a lot of people watching the footage emailed me to express their gratitude. They believed my sole intention at that moment had been to reassure the boys that they were found and that people would soon be working to extract them. Full disclosure: while that was undoubtedly true, there was another, more selfish motive for pushing the idea. *I was trying to convince myself.*

I needed to underline the new reality. Not five minutes earlier, I had been hoping to turn around for home. I was tired, overwhelmed and drained after a tumultuous week, having dived, pulled and crawled through a flooded subterranean maze for hours on end. Now I was presented with the daunting prospect of evacuating a football team of boys through an environment that had already defeated some of the most experienced special forces operators in Thailand, not to mention a number of resilient military divers from around the world.

Considered as a whole, the job certainly should have been beyond Rick and me. As far as we knew, the stranded kids were unable to swim, let alone navigate their way through the challenging and potentially lethal, watery arteries of Tham Luang with its limited visibility and surging currents. They were also malnourished and frail. That meant there was a high chance, given their weakened state, that the water would turn them hypothermic very quickly. The nightmarish scenario that at least one of them would panic underwater was also a major worry. For now, though, I had to compartmentalise my emotions and prepare for a phase of planning. Leaving the Wild Boars with our spare flashlights, Rick and I hugged the children in turn, then headed back into the flood to tell the waiting rescue teams what we had found. But the pair of us had become linked to those starving, frightened kids with one shared thought.

Believe.

It was now my job to turn that belief into something approaching reality.

Thirteen lives depended on it. Luckily, I had thirteen hard-learned lessons to lean upon.

They would eventually prove the difference between success and tragedy.

■ ■ ■

Here is an inescapable reality: at one time or another, all of us will face what might feel like an insurmountable challenge. In my case, I had to help extract those thirteen stricken people from a drowned cave; another individual's test might present itself as something less dramatic, but equally daunting. Maybe they're fighting a life-threatening condition, or returning from a serious physical or emotional injury. It might be that someone has been tasked with organising a project or event of massive importance; or they have decided to take on a potentially overwhelming life change, such as a move abroad or a shift away from their long-term career.

Each person in a moment of this kind will come face-to-face with the risk/reward conundrum: as with my rescue efforts in Thailand, challenges always arrive loaded with consequences, and that can be a cause for worry. The upside is that the rewards for executing such a task can be satisfying, empowering or even life-changing. Luckily, as I've learned through a life spent rescuing stricken individuals and exploring some of the most impenetrable places on the planet, the psychological skills required to succeed are fairly universal and incredibly translatable to the challenges we all face in our lives.

At this point, you might be wondering, 'How can a bloody cave diver help me with some of *my* struggles?' Fair point. But the answer can be found in the very nature of what I do. Typically, cave divers are problem-solvers, fixers, and thinkers. The very idea of swimming into a series of flooded tunnels, entirely unsure of where they might lead or whether they will finish in a tricky dead end with next to no room to turn around, is what excites some people. (Not all, but some. And from what I've learned about myself over the years, I can definitely be bracketed in the 'some' category.) As far as I'm concerned, the appeal is entirely understandable. Cave diving requires an individual to think under pressure to see an idea or plan through to the end. I have spent my time underwater pushing that idea to the limit.

Being part of a cave-rescue team or an exploration group has required me to learn many hard lessons while developing a number of key skills. I have discovered that among the traits required to operate in such a challenging environment is a healthy sense of focus, as well an awareness of the dangers regarding *overfocus*. I've learned to cope with task loading – a situation in which an individual faces a large number of seemingly simple processes at once. If he or she is not careful, the capacity to manage those processes can quickly diminish. Understanding when a challenge is exposing me to unacceptable risk and then immediately changing course has also become important.

The most successful cave divers appreciate the importance of taking responsibility at all times (while handling the fears created by committing to that responsibility). They also know how to break a big problem down into a series of smaller, more manageable events, and I have often leant into the concepts of teamwork and trust, visualisation and rehearsal and the all-important benefits of rest and decompression. These ideas are really tools that every cave diver has to employ if they are to explore and map previously untouched caves, or even rescue a trapped diver. But those same tools can be transferred to any challenge, or a crisis situation away from a cave, where life can be just as turbulent and unpredictable. In the coming chapters I will explain how.

On the surface, *Thirteen Lessons That Saved Thirteen Lives* details exactly how we were able to save the Wild Boars in what was the most challenging rescue mission of my life. But it also reveals a simple-to-follow set of processes that can be used when facing up to any test, big or small. This starts with acceptance. We're all guilty of listening to the subconscious and self-defeating whispers of the Inner Critic; that snide, nagging presence that says: *'But you can't . . .'* And it's a hard voice to ignore, especially when the negative chatter begins during a nerve-wracking moment, such as that first-time house buy, or before a presentation of innovative, but unpopular business ideas. However, to succeed, we must acknowledge the test and its difficulties, and then respond with an affirmative action. Or, in other words, react to the Inner Critic with force and one simple statement: *'Yes, I can!'* And while this is only a first step, and there's plenty of work to complete afterwards, beyond that simple gesture lies a usually transformative moment.

I have come to understand this process well because cave diving has thrust me into some very daunting situations and the most dramatic and testing of events. During potentially life-threatening experiences at depth, I learned about time slicing and how to think by taking one breath at a time. I discovered the pressure of taking responsibility for someone else's life for the first time when supporting my dive partner, Rick, during what would become a nerve-wracking exploration of Saint-Sauveur in France in 2007. The dangers of becoming overfocused became worryingly apparent during my record-breaking exploration dive of Wookey Hole in 2004: having spent my resources working to move a boulder so I could swim even deeper into the cave, I became disorientated and blinded in the dark brown waters. Elsewhere, I experienced moments of self-discovery regarding uncertainty, pressure and stress; I learned about the importance of self-awareness, commitment, and finding value in defeat. Overall, though, there has been discovery in transforming the seemingly impossible into something more achievable. Applying these lessons, and others detailed in this book, helped me to rescue the Wild Boars in Tham Luang.

This achievement in itself proves the power of an education received underwater, because I have never considered myself to be extraordinary in any way. You might have guessed from my photo that I am not the physically overwhelming, war-hero type. I am not one for telling people how to 'crush it' in boardroom meetings, either. Instead, I am a very real example of what happens when sheer willpower meets the statement, *'But I can't . . .'* head on, because I have worked through that tipping point many times myself. I was bullied as a kid and later downtrodden by people who considered me an outsider, or as odd. Because I lacked confidence, for a while I found it hard to accept the thought that I could rise up to any challenge.

Like most people, when life events spiralled out of control, I worked hard to correct those situations as best I could, and with varying degrees of success. But when things did actually go my way, I assumed that luck had played a part, or that my wins were accidental. For a large chunk of my life I believed, wrongly, that other people were better than me (because they'd told me so), and in many ways my story and the lessons I've learned stand as a polar opposite to the type of narratives written by combat veterans, or fearless adventurers operating at the ends of the earth, all of them bulletproof to pain, fear or anxiety.

Eventually I learned that the limiting beliefs I had held about myself were wrong, my mindset having changed after taking up cave diving in the mid-nineties. I acquired the skills required to succeed and my attitude towards what was possible and what wasn't was transformed. As well as breaking those two cave-diving records, I also accepted a challenging role in which I helped to save lives as a volunteer for the South and Mid Wales Cave Rescue Team. It became my responsibility to locate and assist people trapped in horrific circumstances: individuals stranded in eerie, watery underworlds, detached from civilisation, and sometimes starving hungry, hypothermic and panicked. In many ways I had moved past what I thought was possible for a bloke like myself. And it is this ordinary-person perspective that runs through *Thirteen Lessons That Saved Thirteen Lives*.

Why is that view important? Because it shows that everyone has it in them to push past their limits while handling the type of pressurised situations or life events that they might have ordinarily shirked from. In many ways, I'm more Clark Kent than Superman. Think of me as an enabler for anyone trying to cope having been thrown into unexpected and definitely-not-normal circumstances, or as someone who has thrived under extreme pressure and emerged with a series of hard-learned lessons to share.

It is through experiences of this kind that *Thirteen Lessons That Saved Thirteen Lives* can, I hope, help anyone reading it.

When it came to rescuing those twelve kids and their coach in Tham Luang, the odds were stacked against them because many of the personnel sent to help – including the Thai Navy SEALs – had never been in a cave before. I had considerable caving experience, but unlike the team of elite military operators, I was ordinary. And yet I was able to locate and extract the Wild Boars. That was thanks to the challenges I'd experienced throughout my life, educational events that later proved to me that the first step towards any successful outcome was to respond positively to the Inner Critic that says, '*But you can't . . .*'

The next was to state, against the odds, '*I can.*'

Until, finally, it was possible to say, '*And I have.*'

By applying the processes detailed in *Thirteen Lessons That Saved Thirteen Lives*, everybody has the potential to rise up and succeed with their own challenges. As I've discovered, the results can be startling.

LESSON #1

START WITH *WHY NOT?*

The first steps are always the hardest, and all too often we're guilty of giving up on an idea because the end goal feels daunting. Even when the news had broken that twelve boys and a football coach were stranded in Tham Luang, I initially assumed that joining up with the rescue mission was an unlikely event. Not because the challenge of diving into the floodwaters was beyond me, but because I believed the difficulties of securing permission to work would be too great. It was only once I had asked the question, 'Why not?' and stopped thinking negatively that I was able to involve myself in the search and rescue mission. Without that one simple action, there's every chance the operation might not have been concluded so successfully . . .

DAY ONE
TUESDAY 26 JUNE 2018

The British newspaper headlines on 26 June 2018 made for bleak reading. Around a dozen kids from the Wild Boars football team and their coach were missing somewhere in the Tham Luang caves in Thailand. A storm had surged into the area, bringing with it an outbreak of heavy rain and the downpour had caused the tunnels in the caves to flood. Worse, nobody knew just how far into the mountains the group had travelled, and there was a real concern they might already have drowned. I scanned more and more news sites for any details about the search and rescue efforts. As somebody who had worked on such operations, I wanted to know who was on the ground and how they were functioning, and by the looks of things a mission was very much underway. Sadly, the weather conditions were worsening and there was speculation that a body recovery job might have to take place. I sighed. Whether they had survived or not, the work required to extract those kids was bound to be grim.

Thirty years of experience had taught me just as much. I had previously been asked to enter caves with the aim of bringing both the dead and the living to the surface, so I understood just how unpredictable the work in Thailand could be. My introduction to the sport of caving took place with the Scouts when I was a fourteen-year-old kid, exploring Swildon's Hole, a vast cave in the Mendip Hills, Somerset, that stands at around

9,144 metres in length. When it was first announced we'd be exploring the interlinking tunnels that curved into the hillside I felt excited. I had heard the terrain made for a challenging adventure and was accessed via a ladder set alongside a 6-metre-high waterfall. When the time came to go inside, the descent of the ladder felt bloody agonising. I had a slight build back then, and my muscles ached and trembled as I clung onto the rungs. Even though I was attached to a safety harness, I needed every ounce of strength not to fall off.

Once beyond this obstacle, our group climbed up and down a vertical tunnel called The Greasy Chimney and across a flat slab of rock positioned just above the infamous Blue Pencil Passage. However, the most challenging obstacles were three ducks[*] called The Troubles. The water level inside each one had to be lowered laboriously with a bailout bucket, though this was only half the job. Once at the entrance, the explorer then had to inch their way through the darkness on their back, while 'kissing' the ceiling in order to access the diminishing air pocket above. Once inside, the water rose all around them. The environment was intimidating, but I loved the challenge. Every obstacle was a rush and each test furthered my love for exploration.

My interest was amplified when, at our furthest point underground, the instructor for the day spun us a very tall tale of the challenges of overcoming Sump Two – a 6-metre-long, water-filled passage. He then went on to explain how it was a daunting task, even for an experienced caver, and that a bunch of Scouts like us should forget it.

---

[*] A duck is a submerged tunnel with a tiny airspace at the top.

'Anyone hoping to get through needs to lay in the water for twenty minutes first,' he said, 'That way they can adjust to the very cold temperatures. It's virtually impossible. There's no way I'm taking you in there . . .'

At first, I took his warnings as fact, but not for long. He'd clearly been exaggerating, and the more I heard about the techniques required to make it through Sump Two, the more I felt compelled to return one day.

'That sounds like a challenge,' I thought. 'I'd like to do that once I've picked up some more diving skills.'

Having accepted my return as inevitable, I eventually learned the techniques required to succeed. I loved caving and became obsessed with the idea of cave diving, too; physically I was able to manage the effort because I was into climbing and hiking with the Scouts. But most of all I enjoyed the assault-course nature of overcoming obstacles in and out of water. In many ways, caving served as a great leveller at a time when I was immature, both physically and mentally – suddenly I could do things that a lot of the other kids couldn't. It felt exciting and I continued the sport with the Venture Scouts and into my twenties. Still, when my trip to the much-hyped challenges of Swildon's Hole's second sump arrived twelve years later, it wasn't to be the death trap it had been made out to be – but it was no cakewalk either.

For the exploration, I had borrowed an old fish-bowl diving mask, the type worn by the famous explorer and conservationist Jacques Cousteau, and attached a light to the side. At that point in my life I had only really explored dry caves and this was the first time I'd ever felt like a real diver. In that regard, pulling my way through the dark, muddy water of Sump Two along a fixed rope would prove extremely committing, because this was a 'breath-hold' dive – I wasn't using a scuba tank – and the effort seemed loaded with risk. Nervously, I submerged, pulling frantically on the guide rope.

Those challenges I'd been warned about as a teenage Scout very quickly became apparent. The tunnel could only have been around 60 centimetres high and it was hard not to feel a little claustrophobic as I wriggled inside. I moved along the rope quickly, making an effort to conserve oxygen, but the work was intense – I had to ensure that every handhold was firm and purposeful. If I lost my grip at any point, I would quickly become disorientated and then I'd be in serious trouble.

Bang! Suddenly, my helmet cracked into a jagged outcrop in the roof, an obstacle known to divers familiar with Swildon's Hole. I'd been forewarned that the only way to push ahead at that point was to force myself further down into the silty water. With my breath running out, there was really no time to waste. I swam quickly, pulling myself through a small squeeze in the rock before rising up on the other side and emerging in a pocket of air. The manoeuvre was nerve-wracking. But able to stand in the waist-deep water and breathe, I realised I'd been presented with an obstacle that was apparently beyond me, and had succeeded. *I was past Sump Two.*

There was no way I planned on going any further. An even more remote part of the cave lay ahead and if I landed myself in any trouble between the second and third sumps, help would be a long time coming. But just as daunting was the effort required to get home, and I needed to repeat my nerve-wracking journey through the tunnel. I had struck against my psychological limits. Feeling as if there was very little choice in the matter, I turned around for the entrance.

My adventurous spirit was roused. I later climbed mountains in the Alps and explored American peaks such as El Capitan, the largest rockface in the Yosemite Valley, where I was able to understand and rationalise risk. But as far as I was concerned, the real adventure could be found underground. Cave diving was exploration in the purest sense. *Why?* Well, when Neil Armstrong landed on the moon, a flight path from Florida to the Sea of Tranquility had been plotted by rocket scientists to take him there. Likewise, when Sir Edmund Hillary and Tenzing Norgay summited Everest for the first time in 1953, they only had to look up to know where to go, roughly. They still had to pass through the dangerous Khumbu Icefall and across the sheer rock wall that would later become known as the Hillary Step, but the end was visible throughout the expedition: *the very top.* Cave diving, on the other hand, felt like the final frontier, because there were no maps, coordinates or visible landmarks to guide an explorer as they swam. In fact, the only way to discover what was around a previously unseen corner, or beyond a sump, was to look. And taking a look meant moving into the dark, or through a tunnel that might lead to nowhere. But the rewards were undeniable. Floating into a part of the earth that had never been seen by another human felt like a true honour.

I also understood that calm thought was needed for a diver to function effectively, especially because the world in which he or she was operating in was similar, in terms of danger, to climbing into the Death Zone – the area above 8,000 metres on a mountain such as K2, where a lack of oxygen strains the major organs to such an extent that rational thought and logical movement can feel almost impossible. Underwater caverns are dark, claustrophobic and intimidating places. A lot of the time, a diver needs to think clearly in order to negotiate the tunnels and waterways ahead. The experience is sometimes disorientating, especially for anyone not familiar with the smothering environment of a submerged labyrinth, and that brings its own risks. A novice might panic in a confined space, run out of air and die, or overestimate their abilities and then find themselves trapped with no way of escaping.

At this point I should point out the difference between cave divers and dry cavers. A cave diver is someone who explores submerged tunnels and caverns, whereas a dry caver works their way through a cave system on foot – or on their backside or stomach, depending upon the terrain. Within the cave-diving scene there are generally two types of explorer. The first comes from a diving background. Their experience of moving underwater begins with deep-water diving or wreck diving, and exploring an underwater cave feels like a logical progression in an exciting sport.

The second type of cave diver comes from the opposite position. They are drawn to cave exploration rather than diving, and their interest hinges upon moving through a dark and mysterious world, some of which can only be accessed by diving into water. The diving is really a means to an end and the discovery of new passages is the aim. I'd very much bracket myself in the second category, though anyone thinking there is technically very little to separate the two groups should know that when cave diving became a recognised sport during the 1940s and 1950s, a number of open-water divers decided to join in. Many of them weren't up to it. After several grim deaths, the cave-diving community closed its ranks to anyone not experienced in caving. This attitude remains in place today in the UK, where dry-caving experience is seen as a pre-requisite for a cave dive.

Over time I developed a cool head under pressure, and once I became more familiar with the fundamentals of cave diving, I thrived. But I was also determined to progress quickly, and I worked to pass my basic open-water diving qualifications and learned how to swim underwater in glasses, which was something I had wrongly assumed was impossible. (I had bought a prescription mask. Beforehand I'd been fine when swimming, but without lenses I found it impossible at depth to read the cylinder contents gauges or dive computer.) Later, I was mentored by a number of more experienced cave divers from the Cave Diving Group, such as Duncan Price, until I had gained enough experience to embark on expeditions of my own. Before long I was exploring caves with friends and pushing past the point in an exploration where other divers had given up due to fear, fatigue, or inexperience. I had tapped into something that allowed me to go beyond the limitations I'd imagined for myself.

Swimming through the pitch-black environment was intimidating. While moving through a shoulder-width tunnel in churning, muddy water, the darkness ahead punctured by a triangle of torch light, it was possible for an inexperienced diver to feel overwhelmed, and staying mentally composed was often a constant battle for novices. But for some reason I was able to overcome those stresses. I found composure; I was able to relax, think and plan my way through a network of watery burrows, keeping my terror in check, pushing past any rational fears I might have felt, and swim deeper into a cave than previous explorers. Not that I was competitive or reckless; I liked working within my limits, and my talents were being noticed. When other people found themselves trapped and unable to extract themselves from a sticky situation, I was sometimes called in to help as part of a rescue team.

Cave rescue in the UK is organised into regional groups overseen by the British Cave Rescue Council. These teams maintain a list of active divers with the skills and nerve to assist in the event of a flooding or cave diving incident – a roll-call of individuals with the ability to extract anyone experiencing trouble in a flooded subterranean environment. It wasn't something I had taken any interest in before, and I certainly wasn't anywhere near the top of the list, but when two dry cavers found themselves cut off by floodwaters in Dan-yr-Ogof in South Wales in 2008, I was called in to assist with the work. Alongside two others, I helped them to escape.

During that one incident, I learned that cave rescues really weren't glamorous at all. In fact, there were all manner of stresses and miserableness to overcome if a diver was to succeed. It also became clear that rescue dives tended to happen at the worst possible moments. Cavers usually weren't trapped during a warm, sunny day; they were often reported missing in the middle of the night when the rain was pissing down, and over several years, I was called into action on occasions when staying indoors with a film and a takeaway felt like a preferable way to spend an evening. Dan-yr-Ogof was my first taste of such an event. When our rescue team arrived on site, the cave had already fully flooded and the currents in the main passage were so strong it was impossible to swim against them. It was time to plan.

The best way forward, I realised, was to pull myself along the floor, dragging a line reel with me, all the while moving between eddies, or sheltering from the currents by positioning myself behind an underwater boulder. By the time I had reached the stranded cavers, it was clear the flood was subsiding and after diving a dry tube with hot drinks and food to their location, we waited for the waters to drop, swimming out as a group once a small airspace had appeared. My first rescue had been a good one, and it was certainly an interesting introduction to what I could expect in later events. But, weirdly, there was no overwhelming emotion afterwards. I was simply happy that I hadn't let the side down or dropped the ball. The same sense of relief and quiet satisfaction followed every successful rescue dive from then on. More than anything, that operation in Dan-yr-Ogof proved that I had it in me to meet the challenges of a rescue head-on. I had also made a difference in a very dangerous event. That realisation would pave the way for what was to come.

As my exploration dives became more complex and achieving the objective became increasingly difficult, it was clear that I had what I have often referred to as a good *hit rate*. If that sounds odd, let me elaborate: long and complex explorations have plenty of moving parts to consider, and a lot has to go right if a diver is to extend the known limits of a cave system. Whenever I made it to the end of a cave, or reached an intended target during a dive, I called that achievement a *hit*. During a dive, any number of completely valid reasons to turn around can present themselves, but I've found that I have often been able to solve them and continue safely onwards. (Though I would never criticise a diver for turning around at any point for any reason. I've named a failed dive as a *miss*, but that's disingenuous. Personal safety should always come first.)

In that respect, I've developed a good hit rate. And in a rescue situation what is really needed is a collective of divers with the experience and capabilities to start the job quickly: without too much faffing around they can arrive on site, understand what's required of them and achieve their targets first time, every time. But that style of work can be gruelling and intense, and in those situations, I have found it easier to adopt a particularly dark sense of humour, rather than complaining or adopting a pessimistic position, which is often the quickest route to failure.

There were other factors that set divers like me apart from a lot of the others. The first was that I remained focused, not only on the job in hand, but on my own personal survival. Safety was my priority and I very much understood the importance of *not being a hero*. I had read countless tales of mountain climbers who had died because they were trying to save the life of another mountaineer, one that was actually beyond saving. In desperation, they spent too long working on a negative situation that couldn't be rectified until, eventually, they themselves succumbed to an unpleasant, altitude-related medical condition. While I felt incredibly comfortable underwater, I was also acutely aware of the margins for error and so I kept a keen sense of just how close to death I was during every rescue attempt or exploration.

The second factor hinged on efficiency. I was quick, able to move from sump to sump at speed without too much trouble, and I often configured my kit before a dive in such a way that it was possible to swim through an area of water before climbing out again and scrabbling over a series of boulders, or a waterfall, to make the next sump. For some divers, just the simple process of arranging their air cylinders and mask in those situations could prove time-consuming. I effectively managed to reduce those fiddly moments to twenty seconds or so, and I wasn't one for hanging about. All of those skills made me the perfect

LESSON #5

ONE BREATH AT A TIME

It's easy to feel panicked underwater. Passages can narrow into claustrophobic dead ends. Equipment can fail at the worst possible moment. And a faulty rebreather, or a broken scooter can leave a cave diver making a headlong dash for the nearest airspace as their oxygen supply dwindles. It is essential to remain calm under pressure. Easier said than done, I know, but by utilising one simple technique it is possible to dissect a huge problem into something more manageable, just by working towards three distinct timescales – three seconds, three minutes, and three hours . . .

DAY SEVEN (PART ONE)
MONDAY 2 JULY 2018

W e could have turned around. *Really, we should have turned around.* Four hours into the dive, it was clear to both Rick and me that we were approaching the limits of how far we were able to go given the air remaining in our cylinders. When I checked the gauge, my first third of air was close to expiring. There was no question that we had to consider readying ourselves for the long push back, yet still we swam on through sumps five, six and seven, around 2 kilometres into Tham Luang, laying guidelines, all the while looking out for bodies in the water or some sign of life among the rocky banks. With hindsight, pushing ourselves to an acceptable edge was the right thing to do. In the moment, though, I felt edgy.

Ominous shadows seemed to drift and bob in the water around me, many of them human-shaped. At one point, in what I thought was the lowest part of the cave, I caught sight of some teenager-sized forms above me. My heart sank. *Was it some of the kids?* But having moved closer, I was able to pick out the curved edges of a body board, and then another. I counted four or five. They must have been used by a group of cavers who hadn't been able to swim across the lake that gathered here during dry season. When water had filled this particular section of Tham Luang, the polystyrene boards had risen with it and they were now pinned to the roof in an eerie reminder of the storms raging outside.

At times, it was difficult to know which way to go, or how to navigate the underwater terrain. We were in unfamiliar territory, without a line to follow. As the ceiling rose in one section of the cave, a rock shelf angled up from the muddy floor and we had to crawl through what were shallows ahead. I used the water to buoy the equipment hanging about my body. After about 10 metres, I belly-flopped like a seal into the deeper pools and swam on. Later, in the pitch darkness, I wafted a hand and watched for how the sediment reacted around us. We were supposed to be working our way upstream into the hill. Determining downstream by checking the drifting particles, we'd then swim in the opposite direction into the main flow and hopefully towards a deeper chamber inside Tham Luang.

We pushed into a swirl chamber. This was unknown territory; neither of us had been this deep into the tunnels before, and our plan that day had been to look for Pattaya Beach, an area located somewhere around the eighth chamber in the cave system and a spot where the authorities believed the boys might have found shelter.

I had around 30 metres of thick climbing rope still to spool out. The Thai Navy SEALs had been using it as a guideline and it was stuffed into a fertiliser bag. I'd also been carrying another 200 metres of polypropylene line to fix, the type usually used for UK explorations, and knowing that Rick wasn't going to suggest that we head back first (because he rarely did), I had planned on returning to the entrance after laying all of my line. At that point we would have no choice: to continue without a guideline was unthinkable. Mentally, there was a scheme in place and while we weren't breaking any self-established rules, we were definitely bending them. Rick and I had both passed the point of being able to exit the cave alone in the event of a mishap. We were dependent on one another, and the strong supporting currents on the way back to make a speedy exit before our air supply expired. The clock was ticking.

I focused on physiological control. During moments of last resort, I knew that one method of extending the air supply when moving underwater was 'skip breathing', in which a diver short on air pauses at the end of every inhalation, in effect taking one breath in the time usually used for two. Theoretically, this technique can help extend the air supply, and by a considerable amount, too. Meanwhile, if the same individual can visualise a more relaxed situation – at home, on a beach, or in the garden – it is also possible for them to slow their heart rate. I paused for a few seconds at the top and bottom of every breath. And swimming on into the blackness we followed an ascending cave roof into a new space, passing what turned out to be a 350-metre-long passage, the largest flooded section of Tham Luang.

There was a very good reason for navigating a search dive by looking up and directly ahead rather than simply following the floor: we didn't want to miss any air pockets. Cave explorers are notorious for looking down, rather than up. In what has now become a famous search and rescue story, a cave diver in France once ran out of air and swam into a 'kicking water air bell', a dome-shaped air pocket above a vast, water-filled cavern. To alert any rescuers below, he smartly lowered his mask down to the cave floor on a line, the idea being that it might cause anyone swimming by to glance up. Happily, Frank Vasseur, the diver sent to look for him, understood the message. Upon discovering the mask, he followed the line to find a shaken, cold, but very relieved diver, who would almost certainly have perished had he relied on the search party to glance up at the right moment. While it was unlikely the Wild Boars had been stuck in a similar predicament, we weren't taking any chances.

Still, my apprehension was rising palpably with each passing breath; every inhalation and exhalation seemed to move in lockstep with an inner monologue.

'We should turn round soon,' I thought. *'We really need to turn round soon . . .'*

This urge was offset by a strong resolve to continue; it might have even been intuition, and I hadn't yet uttered those famous last words – *it'll be alright.* Though I sensed it wouldn't be long before they came. Luckily, I had a tactic for processing moments of high stress and I had previously planned my way out of potentially sticky situations by 'time-slicing' – a process in which I broke down the key moments ahead into three manageable chunks. Three seconds. Three minutes. Three hours. In other words, I looked to solve my problems in the short, medium and long term. As I peered up through the murky water to the ceiling above, my timeline was becoming clearly defined . . .

Three seconds: *Where's my next breath coming from?* When diving, I played a game in which, from time to time, I tapped at the spare regulator that dangled around my throat like a necklace. Just feeling it in its rightful place reassured me I'd be in great shape should the regulator in my mouth fail and I was left choking on water, which was always a stressful experience, especially if handled poorly. Reminding myself of where my spare was located helped to calm any short-term anxiety.

Three minutes: *How are we going to find the way forward?* The water around us was heavy with silt and visibility was poor. Staying near the ceiling gave me a visual route marker, but the overhanging rocks made for tricky work when pushing forwards and I had to weave between them by changing course and depth. I was also struggling to secure the line. It dangled in my hands as I swam. To fix it in position I would have to swim to the floor, either following a suitable stalagmite downwards or finding my way blindly in the dark waters below. As I worked, Rick hung back to check that I had effectively belayed the line, all the while keeping an eye out for anything that might have been taking place at my rear.

Three hours: *How are we going to get back safely?* While worrying, this issue was a little way back in my list of priorities – being unable to breathe, or getting lost in the dark were my most pressing concerns. Having said that, I still had to plan for our return. If something were to go wrong, the natural, human response would be to swim for the entrance as quickly as possible to reach safety, or help.

But bolting to the surface, which was over a kilometre away in this case, is often the worst thing a diver can do. It creates a sense of panic, and the more a diver panics, the quicker they breathe; the quicker they breathe, the faster their air supply is used up, increasing the likelihood that an irreversible mistake will be made. There is also the reality that ascending too quickly might cause a nasty case of the bends.

But if that same diver can work their way through the first three stressful seconds to resolve their most pressing issue, then there is every chance their medium- and long-term problems will be solvable too. In my case, I had to think about breathing first and navigating second. Over a number of years I had also made friends with the sense of fear that could surge through me during a dive, and so I reminded myself of similar situations in which I had successfully negotiated an issue in the past and survived. *I would be OK.* And I was right to remain calm. The passage roof was opening up ahead of us and I could tell there was an air pocket above. We had made our way into the ninth chamber.

Then everything changed in an instant. Rick was sniffing the air; I was too. *Was that the smell of rotting flesh?* I sensed movement in my peripheral vision. There was a noise. And when I turned, our ideas and plans were tipped upside down. *The Wild Boars were alive.* I saw all thirteen of them standing on the bank. And suddenly a new set of problems had been presented to me. My mind raced.

Three seconds: *Take one breath at a time.*

Three minutes: *Were the boys OK?*

Three hours: *Could we make it out in one piece?*

THE POWER OF TIME-SLICING

It is so easy to let circumstances run away with us in a moment of high stress, such as the one we faced that day in Tham Luang. Over thousands of years, human nature and the evolutionary process have primed us to react quickly when danger emerges. Sadly, while that might have kept us alive when trying to outrun a sabre-toothed tiger, our nervous system has since become notorious for making some spectacularly poor choices under pressure. Rather than rationally analysing the situation we're in and making a more considered decision, we sometimes buckle under emotional strain and react inappropriately. One time, during a torrential thunderstorm, my car aquaplaned and rolled on a motorway. The vehicle flipped and skidded, and flipped again, eventually coming to a to halt on its wheels in the middle of the busy fast lane. I checked to see if the passenger alongside me was hurt in any way. She shook her head.

'OK, I'm fine too. That's good . . .'

In an instant, everything changed. I began working through my mental checklist.

Am I badly hurt? No. Good.

Is anyone else badly hurt? No. Also good.

How were we going to check on the passenger in the back seat?

Where are my glasses?

How the hell am I going to get us off this motorway?

But while my friend was physically in good shape, emotionally she was melting down. Without warning, I heard the passenger door open and watched, helplessly, as she staggered around the car towards the back door, oblivious to the fact we had come to rest in the fast lane of the motorway. She had completely forgotten the first rule of any emergency situation: look after yourself first or join the casualty list.

Time-slicing is an invaluable tool in such a crisis. This concept had been drilled into me through twenty years working in computer network engineering, because when a computer runs too many applications at once, it can slow down, or drop some of the tasks it might have been working through. Humans, like computers, also tend to overheat and perform inefficiently when overloaded with stress, or when dealing with too many tasks. Having a traumatic car accident on a motorway, for example, would be enough to send anyone's internal hard drive into chaos. The key to dealing with these moments of overload is to scale the bigger problem down into a series of manageable tasks over set periods of time.

Three seconds: *Am I badly injured? Where am I? Is the situation going to get worse? Take one breath at a time* . . .

Three minutes: *Does anyone else need urgent attention? Can we move? How do we negotiate the traffic so we can get to the side of the road?*

Three hours: *How are we going to get assistance? And what the hell are we going to do for a ride home?*

But the importance of time-slicing really struck home during an exploration in 2002, in the early phases of my cave-diving career. At that time I enjoyed visiting the Lot, a region in southern France that was regarded as a holidaymakers' dream in the summer, with almost guaranteed sunshine, fresh-water beaches and scenery. Underground the region was just as appealing. The limestone landscape, with its exceptionally long and deep waterways, had formed an ideal spot for experienced cavers and cave divers worldwide. When I arrived, I had a challenge in mind: this would be the first time I had ever used a rebreather in such a large network of tunnels and I was hoping to visit the end of a number of renowned caves in the region. I would also be working alone.

The first couple of dives went well and I felt ready to tackle my first major objective, which was to pass the second sump in the Fontaine Saint Georges, an area located beneath the village of Montvalent. This exploration would involve an underwater journey of nearly two kilometres, where I would reach depths of nearly 80 metres, at which point I'd follow the cave to the surface in a series of slow, controlled steps so I could decompress. I would then have to repeat the whole process in reverse on the way back, decompressing out of the cave and towards safety. There was little doubt that my limited experience would be tested while operating at such depths. Timing my journey to the surface would prove challenging too.

Cave divers usually carry large numbers of air cylinders and this dive was no exception. As well as my back-mounted rebreather, I was also hauling five tanks, which had been secured to either side of my body. Swimming with that amount of equipment was slow, so to speed my progress I was using a scooter, and my dive plan was to advance to the top of a gravel slope around one kilometre into the cave. Once there, I would jettison some of the cylinders for a break-glass-in-case-of-emergency decompression on the way back, if I needed to. I would then continue onwards, down the slope, into the lowest depths of Saint Georges, before emerging into a dry passage on the other side. Like a mountaineer having reached the summit, I would then have to reverse the entire process before returning to civilisation in time for a well-earned can of Diet Coke and a custard cream biscuit.

To a lot of people, the very idea of dealing with such a large number of tasks alone in an unfamiliar and underwater environment might have sounded rash, but as far as I was concerned, cave diving was a sport that twinned problem solving with consequences. This was a combination that appealed to me because it sharpened the mind, and created a situation where I was responsible for any choices I might make. For example, if I wanted to build and try out a piece of equipment or test a new procedure, the responsibility was on me and only me. That made the experience all the more real. That's not to say I am an adrenaline junkie – I've long stressed that if ever a diver felt their heart racing, they were doing something very wrong. Instead, I enjoyed committing to a task where any moments of failure carried serious implications. By pushing my personal limits with a rebreather, alone in Fontaine Saint Georges, that philosophy was very much being put into practice. It was bound to be an interesting experience.

At first, the dive seemed to be going well. My equipment was behaving and I reached the 1-kilometre mark quite comfortably, where I dropped off my emergency cylinders as planned. I then spent a couple of minutes mentally preparing for the tasks to come – and there was little margin for error. Operating at a depth of 80 metres, alone in the pitch-black, close to 1.5 kilometres into a flooded cave, required composure. I was definitely out of my comfort zone, but once readied, I pointed my scooter down the slope, pressed the 'on' switch and shot off, following the guideline into the inky abyss.

Everything happens very fast when scootering downhill in an underwater cave. For starters, it's important to follow the guideline – losing sight of the rope or tangling myself up in it would have ruined the dive, if not the whole day. I also had to monitor my rebreather, adjusting the oxygen content of the gas I was inhaling, while adding more gas to ensure there was enough volume to actually draw breath. This would prove a delicate balancing act. Controlling my buoyancy was equally important, and this was done by either adding or venting air from both my drysuit and the secondary wing attached to my back. If all of this sounds complicated, that's because it was. At various moments, the experience felt not too dissimilar to patting my head and rubbing my tummy at exactly the same time.

Getting any one of these tasks wrong had the potential to snowball into chaos: there was every chance my body would become pinned to the passage ceiling, or dumped in a messy landing at the bottom of the slope, where I would find myself lost in a blinding silt cloud, with no idea where the exit was. Most pressingly, I'd likely have a rebreather full of water, so drawing in air would be impossible. As I descended, slowly and cautiously, watching as the numbers on my dive computer ticked up, every increment indicated my increasing depth and a growing commitment to the job. There was no turning back now. I felt the water chill around me.

Handily, I had managed to maintain a fair semblance of control, but having reached the bottom of the cave and levelled out, my exploration took a tricky turn. *The guideline had finished!* I desperately looked around for another line as I whizzed along on the scooter, until I realised it had been severed by previous floods and was now wafting somewhere in the water. Instinctively, I tied on my own line to the frayed end, knowing it would at least help me to relocate a rough path back to the entrance should I need it, but I could feel the panic rising and I worked to push it back down. My head jerked this way and that as I searched the ceiling for some clue as to the whereabouts of a vertical tunnel I knew would take me to the other side of the second sump.

It didn't take me long to realise I had missed the way on. Caves such as Fontaine Saint Georges have a high water flow, in which the rapid currents scour away deposits of really fine silt from the surrounding rock. I could see banks of the stuff every-where and no sign of my escape route. Worse still, even the slightest waft of my dive fins, or a murmur of bubbles from the rebreather, was enough to unsettle the sediment in the water. Muddy clouds smoked about me, reducing the visibility to zero and slowing my progress. But I couldn't waste any more time at this depth because I didn't have the spare cylinders for even more hours of additional decompression, or the capacity in my rebreather. Feeling my heart rate spiking, I retraced my journey and instantly realised my mistake. *I had moved out of the main flow of the cave!* Knowing the way on must be in the roof somewhere, I ascended into what I convinced myself was the correct vertical passage, up in the farthest reaches of the tunnel.

Trouble struck me almost immediately. The passage I had moved into was narrow, barely chest-width, and the visibility had dropped to close to zero. Still, I forced myself upwards, but I had become a human scouring pad in a drainpipe, scraping silt from the walls, which darkened the world around me even more. As the passage started to squeeze me in a claustrophobic bear hug, I was fast becoming entombed. I cursed myself. *Overfocused, inexperienced, task loaded, idiot*! I had gone too far, too quickly. But there was no time to listen to my inner critic. Deciding that one good heave upwards should have seen me into a larger passage above, I pushed. And pushed.

The single rebreather I had been using that day came affixed with two small bags called counter lungs that were attached to my chest. Two electronic controllers were positioned alongside them and they worked to keep me alive: in effect these 'computers' ensured the correct oxygen levels were being maintained in my breathing gas. This arrangement allowed the machine to store and process my exhaled breath, and it was a fairly effective set-up with one major drawback: when the counter lungs were restricted it became impossible for the wearer to breathe out. That carried the potential to create a very precarious situation, especially if a diver became jammed between two surfaces.

I was now in that very precarious situation.

Rather than popping out into a larger passage, my committed heave had jammed me into an even tighter section of the rift. I had been blinded by sediment in the water and the rock walls pinched at my body so tightly that I was unable to breathe. I couldn't move my arms, I could barely wriggle my legs, and my chest was constricted. When I then glanced down, I realised in horror that both the displays on my rebreather's electronic controllers were dead. *Had they been damaged?* The severity of the situation was like a bomb going off in my head. *I'm a mile inside a completely flooded and pitch-black cave. My rebreather's failing and my oxygen supply is about to die. I'm pinned tight, with no real idea where the exit might be and stuck at an extreme depth.*

Even if I was able to resolve each problem individually, which seemed unlikely, I had no idea what level of oxygen was contained in the gas I had been breathing. That meant it was impossible to calculate accurately the amount of time needed to decompress before surfacing. In a brief moment of panic, I imagined a nightmarish case of the bends and the hospital wheelchair* that would await me after many hours of failed and very painful medical treatment. For a moment, my situation seemed hopeless; too many things had gone wrong and recovering from them all felt impossible. I would never again experience the warm sunshine and campsite chat that I'd enjoyed in the Lot earlier that morning.

Somehow, though, I was able to course correct emotionally. Sure, the puzzle I'd found myself in seemed incomprehensible,

---

* Decompression sickness or the bends is divided into two categories: type one is loosely classified as 'simple', or pain only. Type two is more serious and can cause an injury to the central nervous system. In severe cases, damage to the spinal cord can leave a diver with permanently limited mobility and loss of sensation.

like the opening moves in a high-stakes chess match with far too many variables. But if I could prioritise the tasks ahead, dealing with them in the shortest timeframe I could imagine, then maybe I could extricate myself from my jam relatively safely. The first step was to pick a task.

'Easy,' I thought. 'Work out how to breathe, it'll only take three seconds.'

Easing my way down, I found just enough space between my chest and the two rock walls to allow my counter lungs to inflate. The rush of what I hoped was breathable air into my lungs felt like a massive relief.

My second task was then to spend a few seconds figuring out exactly *what* I was breathing. Examining the electronic controllers, I realised that rather than being broken, my thrashing around in the rift had caused the switches to turn off. *They were still working!* I quickly set about restarting the system, a process I knew had to be performed very carefully at such a depth, as it could prove fatal. (Choosing the wrong option on the menu might have flooded the rebreather with oxygen, which would have triggered convulsions and a very unpleasant death.) *But what other choice did I have?* Working through the problem helped me to refocus psychologically. My heart rate was slowing; my breathing felt controlled, and I was able to progress towards a medium-term goal. *Perhaps if I allowed myself to plan three minutes ahead, I'd be able to wriggle down from the rift, locate the guideline and make my way to the exit? At which point I'd figure out my decompression schedule and avoid that bloody wheelchair.*

I had visualised a path to success; the solutions to each problem had arrived one-by-one and with every task completion

I moved slowly, *surely*, towards safety. By the time I had moved down the rift and reached the bottom of the gravel slope once more, my terror had changed to quiet resolve. I knew the decompression schedule on my dive computer would be wrong – the rebreather had been switched off, so the gas I had been breathing wouldn't match what the dive computer had expected. My problem was that I didn't know just how wrong it was. After some convoluted mental arithmetic, I added what I considered to be an appropriate amount of time to my decompression schedule and made my journey back towards the entrance of Fontaine Saint Georges.

As I mentioned in the last chapter, decompression is a meditative process for me. While waiting for the minutes to tick by, I reflected on the events of the past hour, and how I had underestimated the challenge. I realised that attempting to lay a guideline for myself through a cave was much harder than following a path set by another diver. Most importantly, it delivered a severe lesson in just how quickly things could go wrong underwater – and how hard it could be to recover from them. But somehow, *I had*.

Having eventually emerged from decompression unscathed, I decided that from that moment on I would face complex situations in three timeframes: organising problems into three seconds, three minutes and then longer, perhaps three hours or even days. I wouldn't move on to the second set of problems without having sorted out the first. I would split my mental capacity into time slices in advance, much like a computer would. Then, in moments of stress, such as those regarding safety or breathing, I would focus entirely on the urgent priorities, discarding any lower priority tasks if the situation became overwhelming. That way I would increase my chances of surviving unharmed.

I later discovered that this practice could be applied to all manner of stressful events, one of which was the buying of my last house. Whenever I had been in a full-time job in the past, securing a mortgage had seemed relatively easy. In order to find out how much I could borrow against my salary, I only had to hand over a few months' worth of payslips to the broker. But all that changed once I became self-employed. The process was transformed into a contractual wrestling match with all manner of red tape and legalese, and I can remember the sinking feeling of being presented with an inch-thick bundle of paperwork by the postman one morning. Inside were all sorts of forms and contracts that required me to dig up various sets of accounts or documentation, or to perform some display of mathematical gymnastics. The workload ahead was so daunting that it became a struggle to avoid giving up.

'This won't happen,' I thought, despondently. 'I just can't do it.'

Then I remembered my situation in Fontaine Saint Georges. I broke down what felt like an overwhelming and insurmountable problem into a list of tasks in order of priority and worked out whether they needed to be completed in the short, medium or long term.

Three seconds: *One breath at a time . . . Read the first form.*

Three minutes: *OK, now scan through the documents and get a rough idea of what paperwork you'll need in order to apply for this mortgage.*

Three hours: *Call the accountant, get your tax returns from the past few years and do the sums.*

Slowly the forms were filled in. And I bought the house.

The technique really can be applied to just about any nerve-wracking event. Say you are due to give a presentation to your peers, a situation that always causes your palms to sweat and your nights to become restless. It might help to time-slice the situation down into short-, medium- and long-term stages.

Three seconds: *One breath at a time. Relax and remember to speak slowly.*

Three minutes: *Remember the message you're trying to communicate. Use your slides and charts effectively.*

Three hours: *Follow up with the group. Was everything clear? Is there any other documentation to hand out?*

By following this procedure, it's possible to avoid a psychological overload, even during the most challenging of circumstances.

Above all, it's important to remember just one thing: *breathe.*

ONE BREATH AT A TIME: THE CHECKLIST

- Prioritise critical tasks. Start with a breath. (Three seconds.)
- Consider your situation. Make a plan. (Three minutes.)
- Progress towards your goal. Look long term. (Three hours.)

Slowly, the awful truth dawned on me. I said to Rick: 'Those kids are going to have to eat something substantial otherwise they'll be in trouble.'

In that moment, we decided to take ownership of something that *was* in our remit. We were going to swim into the ninth chamber with four large kit bags stuffed with ration packs supplied by the US Air Force, in order to give the Wild Boars their first nutritional meal in ten days. (If you could call it a meal. While it might have been nutritionally adequate, it hardly matched up to a plate of steaming pad thai.) Our only problem was that we had technically been 'grounded' by the authorities, and nobody had yet granted us permission to go back inside the cave.

Perhaps it was time to bend the rules. The US Air Force were on board with our idea, and helped us to prepare the rations by stripping away any unnecessary cardboard packaging. Most of the food would have to be transported wet, so items that were unlikely to survive the journey – such as crackers and teabags – were thrown out, too. We then made it clear to the Thai Navy what we intended to do and proceeded with our plan. They neither stood in our way, nor helped, but given we were taking responsibility for a pressing issue that very few people were prepared to acknowledge even existed, there was no reason for them to kick up a fuss.

When we swam through the cave to chamber nine, it would turn out to be my most taxing dive of the operation so far. The army kit bags I used to transport the ration packs were heavy and unwieldy. Usually, when carrying gear underwater, I liked to make sure of its buoyancy before swimming. Sometimes I would add foam to help with the process. Or, whenever we needed to add ballast to a bag, a lead weight, or even a handful of stones were used. In this case, we'd stuffed the pockets of what was a canvas bag with mud, but our efforts were a little overzealous, and the extra load became too much. I was forced to drag the rations along like an anchor, kicking it up whenever I could with my legs, while attempting to follow the line. It made for exhausting work.

By the time I arrived at chamber six, a dark thought had crossed my mind.

'I'm going to use up all my air at this rate . . . Am I going to get stuck too?'

There were already seventeen individuals stranded in the belly of Tham Luang – the Wild Boars and four Thai Navy Seals. I really didn't want to add to the depressing numbers by remaining trapped inside. Having done some maths, I gestured to Rick that I was considering ditching one of the bags, in the hope that I would reduce my workload, and breathing, by hauling just the one package of food. I calculated there should still be sufficient rations inside to stave off the kids' hunger for a while. But Rick fixed me with a glare that needed little in the way of translation.

You're not dropping either of those bags. Fix the problem.

With some further determined poking and prodding, I managed to remove a little weight. I then strapped the bags together so they moved as one and I could swim ahead more comfortably.

A bizarre scene greeted us when we eventually emerged in chamber nine. A torch was being used to illuminate the inside of the cave, and on the bank there was a hubbub. The kids were playing with the Navy SEALs. A chequerboard had been scrawled with a stick into the sand, where a game of draughts was taking place with two sets of repurposed stones. It reminded me of a primary school set-up where the pupils engaged with their teacher in a fun, outdoor activity. Certainly, everybody inside seemed pleased to see us – the SEALs especially, who had been stuck inside for around twenty-four hours. (And because they probably understood the severity of their predicament better than the boys.) Our food delivery would go some way towards keeping the group alive. Though I reckoned we had transported a week's worth of supplies inside, I told the kids they had to make it last for two.

Much of the group's good mood probably stemmed from a sense of relief. We were able to tell the SEALs that their three colleagues had swum back without too much trouble. Then I passed on a sealed note that had been given to us by their commander, a correspondence we had been told not to read. Rick watched them as they tore open the waterproof packet, sensing the orders that had been given.

'You're coming out last aren't you?' he said.

One of the SEALs nodded. They were not to leave the chamber until the boys had been brought back to safety. That meant that if Rick, myself, and the planners above ground, couldn't figure a way of transporting the boys, the SEALs would have to stay there, too, in which case they were highly like to die. But that wasn't the half of it. We had been instructed to swim in a package that was being referred to as a 'Special Communications Device', which, once unwrapped, turned out to be nothing more than an Android phone, a piece of kit that had next to no chance of functioning underground.

As we spoke to the kids and made to leave, more secretive notes were written in Thai and stuffed into the pouch. We were being treated as couriers and that annoyed me a bit. It was also hard not to feel a little anxious as to what was being communicated.

Our apprehensions only increased when we returned above ground and caught wind of the style of rescue being considered to move the mission forward. With the help of all the divers in attendance, including ourselves, the Thai Navy had decided that fifty or so SEALS, plus hundreds of air cylinders, were going to be strung throughout the tunnels in a human daisy chain. With this line stretched as far as chamber nine, each boy would then be passed through the flooded caverns and body-wide squeezes until they were planted safely on terra firma.

Having learned of the scheme, I felt dismayed. There simply weren't enough divers capable of making their way into the farthest reaches of the caverns, as the SEALs had already proved. Meanwhile, the very idea of passing the children back through Tham Luang via a chain of people was a flight of fantasy. Some of the chambers were just too hazardous to hang around in. The plan was never going to work in a million years. Events only came to a head later that day when, during an informal gathering, a Thai official claimed that the situation was under control. As far as he was concerned, a solid scheme was taking shape. 'It's all going well,' he said, inaccurately.

I couldn't believe what I was overhearing. 'No, it's not,' I blurted out. 'The kids are completely fucked and they're all going to die.'

A murmur of shock rippled through the various members of management who were also present. As far as they were concerned, this was brand new information. They certainly hadn't heard anything, *anywhere* that suggested that the current plan wasn't anything other than the best option available. There were disgruntled murmurings. Though our discovery of the kids a day or so previously had seen our cramped quarters upgraded to salubrious, individual hotel rooms, Rick and I were still an unwanted presence. The Thai command did not want to hear that their plan was destined to fail, least of all from us.

Having delivered the unsettling news, our discussions with the Thai authorities continued until gradually, with a little more planning and re-planning, we agreed that the rescue mission could be streamlined further by reducing the numbers of personnel and equipment involved. (With the help of the American Air Force we then reduced them some more.) Finally, the Thai command decided that Rick and I would have to lead the rescue. They realised that nobody else gathered at the entrance of Tham Luang could swim such a number of trapped kids to safety through around 1,500 metres of flooded tunnels, though we were hardly relaxed about the task in hand ourselves. The challenges were so much bigger than anything else we had experienced before. For starters, how would we safely execute such a gruelling mission, especially when it was highly likely that the kids would be terrified and panicked as we pushed them through the flooded caves? And what would happen if some of them died under our care?

Those heavy details, when they were eventually discussed, would leave me feeling more than a little uncomfortable. But for now, at least, we were stepping up.

OWNING IT IN THE REAL WORLD

One of the most powerful tools when taking responsibility is honesty and when facing up to a challenge, we can use it in a number of ways.

So, for example . . .

Honesty of strength: If you are the most able first aider in the group of friends on a hiking trip, take responsibility for administering any medical assistance should it be required.

Honesty of weakness: if your GCSE in Spanish was taken twenty years ago, maybe leave the food ordering to a more linguistically capable friend during a holiday abroad.

Honesty of situation: when things are going horribly wrong, or you're feeling out of your depth in a work project, ask for help, or advice.

Honesty of consequences: if you're going to participate in a sport as dangerous as base-jumping, adopting the 'it-won't-happen-to-me' mindset serves as a flimsy insurance policy. Accept there are risks involved.

Honesty of action: after making a mistake that carries implications for others, own up to it as soon as possible.

I was faced with that very situation after returning from our first food run into the cave. Having deposited my two kit bags of ration packs in chamber nine, I made the heavy return journey to the entrance only to become tangled up in an underwater spider's web of black wire, much of which had been laid in the days before the cave had fully flooded. At that time, the Thai Navy SEALs were attempting to set up a telephone line throughout Tham Luang and I remember thinking then it was just one of a handful of unlikely operations that were being discussed.

Nevertheless, the long shot that it might be possible to communicate via phone inside the tunnels seemed too good to resist, and given the work had gone on regardless, I had no way of knowing whether the cable that held me fast was now unused, or the focus of some ongoing effort. I attempted to wriggle free from the tangle, but it was no good; the wire was irreversibly wound round my leg. My only route out was to cut sightlessly through the wire with my shears. Now free, I continued towards chamber three and the dive base, wrestling with the implications of my actions. Part of me wanted to put my head in the sand, to pretend that it hadn't really happened.

Do I say something? Do I not say something? I might have really fucked up here . . .

I then realised that other divers were possibly swimming into Tham Luang to lay more wire, risking their lives in the process. If a communication line was eventually established, but a malfunction caused by my incident was discovered, somebody would then have to figure out the cause of the problem. A process of that kind could potentially last for days. In the end, I knew I had to do the right thing and admit to my actions.

'This is what I've done. This is where the break is,' I confessed, 'I can go back in and fix it.'

It turned out that the project had been abandoned, but at least I could rest easily, knowing I had done the right thing.

The other temptation, and a failure of responsibility, is not to sweat the small stuff. For example, when you don't read the small print and argue that it's several pages of boring and complicated legalese and that there are more productive ways of spending your time. But that's why so many people get a shock several months down the line when they discover that they have unwittingly committed to an expensive contract, or have locked themselves into an automatic upgrade by mistake. This lazy part of our nature can be so strong that we need to make the effort to retrain our brains. One way of doing so is to focus on the small, fiddly things in everyday life that we can affect, simply by taking responsibility. Such as reading that contract in full. Or checking our insurance hasn't run out. Or making sure our passport has a couple of years on it when booking the next holiday, and so on . . .

The cave diving equivalent to this scenario was highlighted to me during an exploration in the Jura region of France. I was lucky enough to have the backing of a number of French divers who had agreed to provide support by staging equipment at various points throughout the cave. Having other team members position equipment this way can save a tremendous amount of effort. Still, wherever possible, I'm always careful not to commit to a dive without ensuring all the equipment needed for a safe exit is in place. In this case, my support team experienced significant difficulties reaching their pre-agreed drop-off points. On following them in, I became involved in a game of underwater *I-Spy*, as I tried to spot and retrieve the equipment that had been dumped almost at random throughout the early sections of the cave because my support divers weren't able to carry it through.

Incidents of this kind only highlight what have long been personal rules: I always try to take responsibility for myself. I do my best to act with honesty. And I always read the small print. As a result, I know that if I do come to a sticky end when working underwater, there will be nobody else to blame but me.

STEP UP AND STEP BACK: THE CHECKLIST

- Take ownership. Accept responsibility.
- Be realistic. Don't overreach.
- Play to your strengths. Acknowledge your weaknesses.

LESSON #8

HARNESSING TEAMWORK AND TRUST

The concept of trust is a mortal one in cave diving, as it would be in a dangerous vocation such as firefighting. When working in a group, every diver places their life in the hands of others, so it's important that he, or she knows without any doubt that their colleagues can be relied upon. Those connections are often hard to find, or they might take years to establish, which is why Rick Stanton and I have worked so well together in the past. Decades of diving as a duo have created a firm bond – he has my back and I have his. But in order to create trust within a group setting, it's vital the people working together in the collective understand the key elements of teamwork – the sharing of information, collective thinking, the power of controlled ego and the distribution of credit. Only then can they operate together successfully . . .

DAYS EIGHT AND NINE
TUESDAY 3 JULY–WEDNESDAY 4 JULY 2018

- - - - - - - - -

This was shaping up to be the most complex rescue mission I had ever worked on. Thankfully, our efforts were being supported by a collection of military and civilian specialists from Australia, America and Thailand, among others – individuals who were both skilled and effective. However, what was really needed were divers I had worked with previously; people I could trust, because without a strong team connection I would eventually find myself fixed in a constant state of high alert as I worked underwater, worrying about whatever Diver A was doing, or whether Diver B had staged our cylinders in the correct spot. My focus needed to remain at all times on the kids, not to mention on my own safety.

Before we could think about adding to our numbers on the ground, I first had to improve our relations with the local armed forces. While we had undoubtedly established a bond with the Americans, our biggest logistical obstruction was still proving to be the Thai Navy SEALs, or, at least, their superiors. We were constantly being made to feel like an inconvenience, despite our key role in the rescue, but I felt that their cooperation, however difficult to secure, was essential. As a planning team made of Rick and myself, plus senior members of the US Air Force, figured out how best to manoeuvre thirteen people from the ninth chamber, any suggestions from us were dismissed by the authorities; any requests we made were still being greeted with indifference. A strange tension was developing, which I tried to overcome by communicating the details of our plans to the Navy SEALs whenever it seemed appropriate.

Simultaneously, we contacted the British Embassy in Bangkok. It had become clear to us that the divers Jason Mallinson and Chris Jewell, plus support personnel Gary Mitchell and Mike Clayton needed to be working alongside us, as they were people that Rick and I had respected and trusted for years. Jason and Chris were long-term dive partners who I had worked with multiple times over the years – I swam alongside Jason on our record-breaking exploration in Pozo Azul. Importantly, both were dived-up and carried a decade or two of experience in exploring cave-diving terrain similar to the kind we were working through in Tham Luang.

Meanwhile, Mike and Gary were experienced surface controllers. Their role would be to manage everything above ground, which included liaising with the military, coordinating our equipment supplies, and fending off the media. The dive team of Rick and myself, plus Jason and Chris, would be underwater for many hours without any form of contact with surface control. (Conventional radio and smart phone signals simply do not function underground, or underwater.) Mike and Gary would know exactly what to do in those silent hours.

The arrival of all four was arranged in two waves through the British Cave Rescue Council and the Thai embassy in the UK. Jason and Chris showed up within two days, Mike and Gary followed shortly after. We requested the help of three more divers: Josh Bratchley, Jim Warny and Connor Roe. Apparently,

Josh had been abroad when our message for additional assistance had come through and he was flown home and then driven back to the airport again, a police escort steering him the whole way, its blue lights flashing. Connor was more prepared, having readied and packed his gear in anticipation of a phone call.

Rick and I were now working with a group of divers we both knew and trusted. Teamwork and communication would be key, as would our ability to encourage our new teammates to *want* to succeed as much as we did, because I had developed an incredibly strong sense of ownership of the kids' wellbeing and I intended to work to the limits of my personal safety in order to save them. Perhaps irrationally, I believed that nobody was going to commit to the job in the same way as me, though I also understood the impossibility of being a control freak in such a huge operation. More than anything, I felt it was important to give ourselves the best shot at success, no matter what it took.

When selecting a team such as the one we were building in Tham Luang, I had found that it's most important to choose people that I have trusted in the past and then to trust the people I've chosen. As far as I'm concerned, the perfect dive group is one where every individual within it is responsible for their roles, they can operate competently on their own, they are able to look after themselves, and finally, they possess enough capacity and discipline to assist a team-mate or a casualty, especially if disaster strikes. Beyond that, it's important that everybody is happy to work as part of a team and then functions in a selfless manner. Egotism, as I'll discuss later, is a troubling trait in a cave diver.

Overall, though, trust is the most important attribute when working as a team underwater and with it, Rick and I have saved each other's lives several times. On one occasion, in southern

France during 2007, he was eager to dive into unexplored passages in a cave called Saint-Sauveur, in the Dordogne region. The two of us, plus another diver, Rupert Skorupka, had planned to dive separately. On the first day, Rupert and I swam into the furthest known reaches of the cave, familiarising ourselves with the terrain while being supported by Rick. The next day, we swapped with Rick as he attempted to push into unknown territory.

In many ways, we were breaking new ground, technologically speaking. In 2007, it was considered unusual, perhaps even risky, to dive to some of the depths we'd planned for while using rebreathers. There simply hadn't been enough successful cave dives with the equipment we were using to draw conclusions as to which of our procedures would be safe. Rick was aiming to push past 180 metres, a depth that was nearly twice as deep as that reached by the ill-fated Russian submarine, the *Kursk* when it had sunk in the year 2000.

But very little had been written on how to achieve those numbers, not without the logistical support that commercial divers enjoyed*, and we felt that a much more lightweight approach was required. Rick and I had decided to use a different type of rebreather at depth, one we hoped would prevent a lethal build-up of carbon dioxide in our system. We had also developed what we believed were suitable plans and procedures to integrate

---

* Commercial divers or 'saturation divers', such as those working on oil rigs can spend many days in a pressurised environment. They operate from diving bells and have teams of surface support personnel managing their wellbeing; they are always connected to the diving bell by a life support umbilical cord or hose, and have huge banks of oxygen and other gases on hand for emergency purposes. This type of infrastructure simply isn't possible in exploration dives, or the type of rescues I was engaged in, mainly due to the huge expense. The small size and location of most caves was a prohibitive factor too. (Though one exception was the Wakulla 2 Expedition in Florida in 1998, where a diving bell was used to make the hours of decompression more comfortable.)

our rebreathers with the equipment and dive computers we already had. All things considered, it was very much a work in progress.

My first dive was thankfully uneventful. Having reached a depth of around 130 metres, I swam over a kilometre into the cave. *And the rebreather had worked!* But Rick's exploration the following morning was far more colourful. As a support diver, I was required to meet him a couple of hours into the exploration, during his decompression, where I would then help to remove any unwanted equipment while providing moral support. But on making it 250 metres into the cave, I saw no sign of him at the rendezvous point. I ventured another several hundred metres inside, but there was still no sign. An uneasy feeling clawed at my gut. Hours passed; I returned to the surface for air and then made a second fruitless dive but I still couldn't spot Rick anywhere. It was only on my third attempt that I eventually, *thankfully*, located him. He had spent much longer at depth than expected, and though his emotions were in check, he was clearly unhappy. Despite a successful exploration, Rick had used more gas than expected and his breathable supply wasn't likely to last for very long into decompression. He was in a bit of a fix.

Rick wears a black mask, and underwater he has an uncanny ability to deliver a withering stare, usually when the person alongside him is about to do something stupid. I was now on the receiving end of that look. Gesturing me close, Rick asked for my underwater notebook and I wondered what the hell I had done wrong. When he eventually turned the waterproof pages my way, four words had been scrawled on the surface in pencil.

I NEED YOUR REBREATHER.

The demand was unsettling. Divers simply don't exchange gear underwater, especially several hundred metres into a cave, and definitely not at the significant depths we'd found ourselves in. Though I was undoubtedly questioning, despite my reluctance, I trusted Rick and knew he wouldn't have asked me had he not thought a) it was necessary and b) there was no other choice. Another glare left me in little doubt that we were fast approaching crunch point, while at the same time suggesting that the request was completely normal and could be accommodated by just about any fool. (It's funny what just one look can tell you.) I composed myself and then indicated I would need around a minute to fashion a makeshift harness for my cylinders, one that would allow me to exit the cave without my rebreather. Rick was staring again.

You can have a minute . . . but no longer.

As we began the complex process of exchanging equipment, Rupert Skorupka entered the water to see what was happening. As he swam into view, I noticed his eyes. They had been magnified by his dive mask and were as wide as a pair of saucers. To him the scene must have looked like some kind of madness: enough equipment to start a dive school had been strewn all about the passage. Above him, Rick was calmly floating at the ceiling; I was below, lying on the floor, and both of us were adjusting our equipment without actually wearing any of it.

As Rick fiddled with my rebreather, I realised he'd never worked with that particular model before, and therefore had no idea how it might function, not that quibbling over this particular fact seemed very sensible at the time. Furthermore, what I didn't know (and wouldn't discover until surfacing) was that Rick's rebreather had failed and was fast filling with water. We swapped kits and I delivered a brief lesson on his new rebreather unit, distilling the bare essentials of several days' worth of teaching into around ninety seconds. Having got the message, he visibly relaxed and began what would be twelve, long, lonely hours of underwater decompression. With the immediate problem solved, I swam Rick's rebreather to the surface, where I drained away the water inside, replaced the carbon dioxide absorbent and recharged the oxygen cylinders. I then returned it to Rick, whereupon Rupert and I could set about helping him through the night as he continued his slow ascent in stages.

Despite the drama, Rick's exploration of Saint-Sauveur had been successful, because we had trusted each other implicitly. We were a small but effective team. Over ten years later in Tham Luang, the scale of our task demanded a far bigger workforce, and in addition to Jason, Chris, Mike and Gary, we needed a team of support divers to help us set equipment throughout the cave. After Ben Reymenants and his dive partner had departed, a new group of European diving instructors working in Southern Thailand had arrived. Among them were Claus Rasmussen and Ivan Karadzic (both from Denmark), Mikko Paasi (from Finland), and Erik Brown (from Canada). The positive side of their arrival was that the number of technical divers working on the ground had expanded, and given they were also expats living in the south of Thailand, they understood the area and the culture. The negative was that none of them had any experience in working on cave rescues.

When the US Air Force first introduced the group, and insisted we work with them, I was wary. But over the coming days, we assessed their suitability through a series of tasks that would prepare the caverns for the upcoming rescue – they moved lines through the tunnels, tidied up the cave of equipment and discarded cylinders, and cut away some of the inactive wires that had been blocking our path in some of the sumps. We soon nicknamed our new recruits the 'Euro Divers'.

These were relatively low-priority chores. If one of the Euro Divers cocked up, or failed to complete their work, it was of no great consequence, but any blunder would shine a light on who was capable and who wasn't. We had to know which guys delivered on their promises and which ones fell short. Some of the Euro Divers only went into the cave once before deciding the work was not for them. The egotists in the group were noted too. In much the same way that a new line manager likes to assess the staff working around them in a company during their first few weeks in the job, so we were assessing our resources, only we had minutes and hours in which to make that judgment, rather than days and weeks. After several shifts of work, Claus and Mikko proved to be very helpful indeed – they hadn't died and were more than prepared to swim into the caves, over and over. They seemed competent and in control, and I felt confident working alongside them. Both divers would turn out to be useful additions.

The team was in place. Rick and I, plus Jason and Chris would work as lead divers. Mike and Gary were set to run all aboveground communications and logistics, while a mixed team featuring the likes of Josh, Connor, Mikko and Claus would act as support divers, staging air cylinders and other equipment throughout the cave. At various stages we would also rely on members of the American Air Force and Australian Navy. A comprehensive plan wasn't yet in place, but at least we had the crew to tackle the workload ahead.

BEWARE THE EGO

There is little room for ego when exploring caves, though plenty of divers carry one with them and the sport is a magnet for big personalities. But competitive bravado can lead to reckless behaviour and pig-headedness, which can cause all manner of unpleasant scenarios. One of the reasons I've worked well with others is because I have never attempted to compete; proving myself to the people around me isn't my thing. Instead, I am competitive with myself and I am a harsh self-critic. Yet when it comes to presenting myself as an authority figure I'm just not interested.

There was one occasion when my attitude became very apparent. I was diving into a cave in southern France with a colleague called 'David', an experienced cave and commercial diver who was a very accomplished explorer. (For the purposes of this story, I have changed his identity.) David would need all his famed nerve as this cave had a very tricky profile: the passages led us down to depths of around 100 metres before rising up again, and then down, and up, and down again. *It was like a bloody roller coaster.* In decompression terms, this dive was considered a very risky exploration.

We had decided to work as a parallel team, meaning that if one of us turned back for any reason, the other would still continue forwards, and we eventually made it out of the water and into an area of previously unexplored cave. Up until that moment, neither of us had discussed what we should do in the event of breaking new ground, and having got to the point where we were clearly about to do so, I realised the route ahead looked sketchy and that we should tread carefully. We were faced with a

45-degree rock slope that rose out of the water, with a number of dangerous looking drops on the left side. The only way on was to crawl up the slope and then along the tortuously low passage beyond. If one, or both of us, was to become trapped or injured, I knew of very few divers in the world with the ability to rescue us. (And the expense of the amount of beer I'd have to buy Rick, if he was called into action, didn't bear thinking about.)

Then there was the issue of our kit. Both of us were carrying plenty of it, and as we squeezed through a narrow tube in the rock, hoping it would lead into another cavern rather than wedging us tightly inside, the smallest of movements made for heavy work. We had also been wearing drysuits, because the water temperature was freezing cold, but with so much physical effort now taking place out of the water, I realised I was overheating; my skin was covered in sweat, a situation that meant the dive back would be extremely chilly, not to mention the hours spent in decompression afterwards.[*]

Meanwhile, the terrain we were crawling over was strewn with jagged rocks. (Unexplored cave passages are often made up of razor-sharp stone, because nobody has clambered over them, to smooth the surfaces.) The slightest tear to a drysuit would have made it impossible for the wearer to swim back – as I've discussed previously, just the slightest nick would have exposed the diver's skin to a brutally cold underwater environment. To say we were taking a risk at this stage in the exploration was an understatement.

---

[*] Drysuits keep out the water, but when a cave diver is soaked with sweat, the thermal layers underneath become damp. In icy temperatures, hanging around in wet garments can lead to hypothermia.

But David wanted to be the first into the next stretch of water, to make his mark on the cave. Or at least, that's how it looked to me. As we continued our exploration, he surged ahead, still carrying his kit with him. Suddenly, an awful realisation dawned upon me.

'He wants to go first. He wants to go the furthest. *He's bloody charging ahead!*'

It wasn't a game I wanted to play. And as I watched David rushing on, a showreel of potential disasters played out in my head. By carrying so much kit at speed, over this unstable terrain, he could easily fall, twist an ankle or break an arm.

And then . . . *near disaster!*

While scaling a muddy bank, he slipped. David's backside slid out from underneath him and he skidded and tumbled down the gradient for around 10 metres before landing in a pool of water. It was a relief to see him unhurt, but I understood even more clearly that rushing in an environment of this kind was foolhardy. What had mattered to me was that we succeeded as a team. I certainly wasn't exploring this cave for personal glory, and I had no real desire to be the first one past whatever imaginary finishing line lay ahead.

I had long known that one technique for preventing a big personality – even an overbearing ego – from imploding is to slow down the situation they are working in. During a business meeting, for example, a work colleague might become too confrontational, or appear eager to press ahead with an idea that others in the team are unsure of, or resistant to. In those instances it helps to take a break, or to call a timeout to slow the pace of a dispute that might otherwise spiral out of control. I had to employ a similar tactic with David.

In desperation, I called out, hoping to simmer him down a little. 'Wait! I'll carry your equipment for you,' I shouted.

The shift in our momentum was almost instantaneous. David, suddenly stripped of any competition, dropped gears, knowing that he would be the first diver into the next sump or chamber. Having shared his load between us and settled what had looked to me like a race, we successfully found and explored the next sump without too much drama.

Taking the backseat in a team environment is often the best tactic to adopt when a bullish personality is determined to drive everybody forwards at any cost. That's not to say we should become passive, or blindly follow a reckless or overly ambitious leader. Instead, we should use our influence to control the situation subtly, so that everybody feels pleased with the eventual outcome. Often, I have likened this situation to working on an old sailing ship, where a strong character, absolutely determined to lead the way, takes charge as captain.

Having expressed a determination to steer, and knowing that the direction is roughly the correct one, it helps if the other crew members are willing to park their egos, working around the big personality in question in such a way that the overall objective is achieved satisfactorily. As the self-appointed captain presses forward, his crew should keep an eye on what is happening at the side of the vessel, or check the compass, and scan the horizon for other boats. Really, there's no need for the others to attempt to stamp their authority on a situation while the ship is heading in the right direction. And if, for some reason, things start taking a turn for the worse, the attentive crew will be the first to know. From there, they can work through the issues in play with their captain.

Too often, the opposite happens; a team of personalities, unhappy at being led, or at having their egos challenged, clash in such a way that an ugly power struggle breaks out. I have seen this all too often when watching the reality TV show, *The Apprentice*. During the weekly group challenges, where a number of hopefuls attempt to catch Lord Alan Sugar's eye with their creative business acumen, a hierarchy is often arranged in advance; one contestant is installed at random as team leader. But what happens next is often the exact opposite to what should occur on my imagined ship. Crew members rarely check the sides of the boat. No one takes responsibility for the compass. The horizon is left unchecked. Instead a war of personalities kicks off in which the more egotistical members of the group vie for leadership, while undermining any potential successes they might have shared. It is a complete waste of time for everyone, though there's no denying it makes for entertaining TV.

Interestingly, there is a technique for those leaders who know they have a big personality (and also those without one), and it can be used to overcome any simmering tension their ego might be causing. It is well known that one of the key traits of an alpha character is the overwhelming desire to take charge, or to lead in whatever's going on, whether that be in sport, a social activity, business or sometimes family life. However, in those environments, when feelings can be hurt and plans can be derailed, one way for leaders to create respect and understanding is by simply sharing the credit within the group whenever success comes their way. In the case of *The Apprentice*, any team leader that publicly acknowledges the efforts of their teammates – the ones who so ably contributed to the overall work – will find their colleagues more agreeable to helping out next time around. Likewise, taking one for the team, or accepting responsibility when things don't work out as planned is often repaid with respect and loyalty.

There have been situations where I have been forced to take the lead, and I've found this same technique to be very helpful when bringing a team together. For example, while working in Tham Luang, our dive team received requests to give media interviews. During the rescue, we firmly refused. Afterwards, however, during conversations with journalists, we generally made sure to stress that our efforts to save the Wild Boars had been conducted as an 'International Team'. Deflecting the credit away from individuals and pushing it towards the group seemed a good way of making sure that everyone's contributions were acknowledged.

It was a technique I tried to use after the rescue, when our group of motley divers was invited to Downing Street to meet with the former prime minister, Theresa May. Sadly, Rick was unable to make it and the responsibility for explaining the events that had unfolded in Tham Luang was placed firmly on my shoulders. Throughout the conversation, I made sure to introduce the others in the team and then to spread the credit equally among the group. To my frustration, Mrs May continually fired the attention back at me, until our chat resembled a tennis rally, though I think my teammates appreciated the effort. (The undoubted highlight of the visit was watching Matthew, my twelve-year-old son and guest for the day, as he sat in the PM's chair in the Cabinet Room like he owned the place. He then polished off more than his fair share of cake.) As a person, I'm generally validated internally, and though I like the respect of my peers, I don't *need* it. I have always felt that respect and trust are earned, rather than bought, or built by bullying. As far as I'm concerned, leaders achieve much better results by under-promising and over-delivering, by being respectful and reliable, and by working towards a group goal. It is not vital for them to always steer the ship – or grab the glory.

HARNESSING TEAMWORK AND TRUST: THE CHECKLIST

- Select those you trust. Trust those you select.
- Share information. Respect viewpoints.
- Delegate responsibility. Steer only when necessary.

LESSON #9

HURRY UP AND DO . . . *NOTHING*

Sometimes when a crisis situation develops around us, it's tempting to want to rush into action and to fix things. (And to fix things now!) However, the reality is that some crisis events play out like a game of chess in which rushing headlong into a poorly thought-out plan of attack, or defence, can be the worst thing to do – mistakes are made, key pieces are lost and accidents happen along the way. Through rushing we find ourselves manoeuvred into checkmate.

Instead, it's sometimes better that we hurry up and do . . . nothing. I know this sounds counter-intuitive, but by pausing for breath in the first three seconds of a dispute, accident, or failed plan (see Lesson #5), or by making a little room to think in a situation where the clock isn't against us, we can plot our escape away from trouble, all the while using haste rather than speed . . .

DAYS TEN AND ELEVEN
THURSDAY 5 JULY–FRIDAY 6 JULY 2018

Tragedy had struck.

I could tell something was wrong as soon as we arrived at the entrance to the cave that morning. The mood was subdued; the emotional impetus had faded, and there was very little evidence of the enthusiasm created by the discovery of the Wild Boars just a couple of days earlier. *But what the hell had happened?* Having spoken to a handful of engineers around us, the grim truth about the dangers of cave diving was confirmed. One of the rescuers, a former Thai Navy SEAL named Saman Gunan, had died somewhere in Tham Luang. The news came as a terrible blow.

From what I knew about Saman, he was aged thirty-eight, an athletic bloke, and physically capable enough to cope with the rigours of a gruelling penetration into the caves. However, superior physical fitness counted for very little when negotiating a flooded passage or managing the air supply required for a difficult round trip. It was the latter that had scuppered Saman, and during the return leg, tragically, he had run out of air and drowned. Perhaps a lack of recent experience had been the vital factor: Saman was a volunteer, and having left the Thai Navy SEALs in 2006, he had gone on to work as a patrol officer at Bangkok's Suvarnabhumi Airport. That hadn't diminished his enthusiasm for an against-all-odds challenge, though, and after learning of the Wild Boars' predicament, he had decided to help with the rescue efforts.

While the exact order of events and some of the details surrounding his death are a mystery, the broader outlines of what had happened sounded sadly familiar to anyone associated with cave diving. Saman had swum to some of the deeper reaches of the cave, beyond chamber five, with a haul of oxygen cylinders. By the sounds of things, there hadn't been too many problems on the way in. But on the return trip, his dive buddy turned around to check that everything was OK, only to find Saman had slipped into unconsciousness. First aid was delivered and Saman was transported to dive base in chamber three, where he was given CPR, but nothing could be done. He was gone. After Governor Narongsak relayed the news to the workforce at Tham Luang, the buzz and optimism that had been charging through the camp fizzed away like a sigh of air from a punctured tyre.

A great deal of speculation can swirl around during the frantic hours and days following a diver's death. *Could anything have been done differently to prevent Saman's accident? Was his equipment at fault? Had he misread the measurements on his cylinder contents gauge?* These curiosities are usually put to rest by a thorough investigation of the incident, but any information that might have been drawn from such an investigation wasn't shared. I found that a little unsettling. If, for example, Saman's drowning had been caused by a bad air fill, one that contained carbon monoxide from the compressor exhaust, then a wider problem might have been in play: his tank could have been one of a bad batch of air cylinders, meaning every diver on site was playing a worrying game of Russian roulette as they inhaled from their regulators. However, the most logical assessment was that Saman had died having run out of air. I felt desperately sad for his friends and family, and it was yet another reminder of the high stakes nearly constantly at hand.

We had to move on; there was no time to dwell on the loss. Part of our work now involved familiarising our newly assembled dive team, which included Jason, Chris, Jim and the Euro Divers, with the deeper recesses of Tham Luang, and there was plenty to learn. Swimming in to chambers three, four and five was one thing. Getting to the final cavern was an entirely different kettle of fish, and it would take nerve, stamina and skill to get there. Our new arrivals were fresh and physically up to the task, but I worried that the difficulty of the rescue and the involvement of children could create an emotional fallout if things went wrong – I had noticed that with each run into the ninth cavern, our connection with both the boys and the SEALs was growing. Sometimes, I found it hard to detach myself psychologically from what could prove to be a very painful and depressing conclusion. The thought of any of the kids dying, especially one that might have been directly in my care, was deeply concerning. If there was a chance I could minimise any potential mental anguish for my teammates, I was eager to do so. (Though cave divers aren't renowned for sharing their inner thoughts. We can be a pretty closed-off bunch.)

I was most concerned for Chris. Behind Rick, Jason and I, he was the most experienced diver on the ground, even though he was yet to prove himself in a real rescue. For this reason, it was important he familiarised himself with the cave before the extraction of the Wild Boars got underway. He wanted to meet the kids, but I worried that his enthusiasm had caused him to overlook the potential emotional consequences. With hindsight, I don't think he understood the seriousness of what he was getting into, and by swimming in to chamber nine in advance, he was only going to bond with a group of people who had a very slim chance of surviving the eventual rescue operation. I guess his emotions might have been running hot. As an officer of the British Cave Rescue Council, he had become a spokesperson on the Tham Luang rescue at home. Now transported to Thailand and part of the team for real, he was eager to pull his weight and prove his worth.

At one point, Rick even asked Chris if he was certain of his actions. 'If you go in, you might be one of the last to see these children alive,' he said. 'Are you sure that's what you want?'

Chris nodded and pressed on into the cave with Jason for their first run. I watched him go, hoping he wouldn't come to regret the experience.

In the end, both divers were able to make it to the Wild Boars without too much incident. And having handed over the latest run of supplies, they decided to hatch another plan. A series of notes, written by the kids' parents, had been carried in with the ration packs. While watching the boys' faces as they read through their letters, every missive full of love and support and hope, Jason wondered if there was any value in encouraging the Wild Boars to reciprocate the gesture. Handing over a pencil, he instructed everybody to scribble down replies of their own. His hope was that their words might lift the spirits of the frazzled families waiting outside.

The pages brimmed with optimism. All the children told their parents they loved them; others spoke of being excited at leaving the caves. Titan even placed a dinner order for when he eventually made it home. 'Please tell Pee Yod, get ready to take me to eat fried chicken.'

'I am fine,' wrote Dom. 'It is a bit cold, but don't worry. Please don't forget my birthday.'

Coach Ek put together a note in which he told his grandmother not to worry, before pencilling an apology to the families expressing his sorrow at the Wild Boars' predicament: *To all kids' parents, at this moment, kids are well. They have teammates who are bigger to take care of them. I promise you that I will do my best to take care of them. I would like to thank you for moral support and I apologise to all parents.'* Given the age of the kids stuck in the cave, it was easy to forget that at twenty-five, Ek had not long been a grown-up himself.

While the letters were certainly morale-boosting, our team had a job to do, and we had to do it well. I needed to shut out any external white noise and focus on the task in hand, but the reconnaissance effort brought a new message from the military trapped inside. The four SEALs had claimed they could hear the sound of snorting pigs and squawking chickens from the depths of Tham Luang. Drawing from that incredibly flimsy evidence, the Thai authorities began to direct their attention towards any farms that were located in the area. Their hope was that an open shaft might be found somewhere above chamber nine. After all, what else could explain those farmyard animal noises ricocheting into the caves?

But life underground can be a disorientating experience, especially for someone who has been trapped in very uncomfortable circumstances for days. Lights will flash and flicker in the distance, even though there is nobody else around. As water flows through the tunnels it's also possible to hear strange noises and voices, sometimes as murmurs – sentences and names that echo eerily through the darkness. Each one raises the hope that help is on its way, but they are usually nothing more than a hallucination. The experience isn't too dissimilar to those excitable moments spent waiting for a mate, or a loved one, at a train station on a gloomy winter evening. Every face or silhouette that walks through the ticket office as the latest commuter train pulls in – their collars turned up, hands shoved into pockets – can resemble the person you're waiting for until the truth is revealed from a distance of 30 metres or so. Hundreds of people turn out to be nothing more than a false promise.

But hearing things is totally normal in a cave. Divers understand this reality; stranded and scared individuals with no real experience of operating underground rarely do, and so the Thai military had become convinced that a search should be made for some imagined menagerie of livestock when all that was above the Wild Boars was a vast expanse of jungle and nearly a kilometre of mountain rock.

My best course of action was to wait and prepare – *and to hurry up and do nothing*. It seemed like the smartest choice under the circumstances. From my perspective, all that could be done was being done. Chris and Jason were familiarising themselves with the cave and taking in supplies. The Euro Divers were working on their own preparations; the equipment we needed was being sourced and readied; and our infrastructure was coming together nicely. Any fussing or micro-management on my part wasn't going to help. Alongside Rick, I took a moment to rest and recover, and then to ready the best possible plan to rescue those kids.

THERE'S NO SUCH THING AS A ZERO-RISK OPTION

As we went to work on figuring out just how we were going to extract the Wild Boars, Governor Narongsak made a bold proclamation. When it came to any suggestion tabled by the various rescue teams, he would only accept a 'zero-risk plan'. By that, I took it to mean that if there were the slightest chance that somebody might die during the process – whether that person be a SEAL, a diver, or a Wild Boar – then the operation would be scrapped and the brainstorming would begin again. I remember rolling my eyes on hearing his announcement. Every action in life, let alone in a cave rescue, comes with some form of risk attached.

There was also the reality of our situation to consider. Given there was no such thing as a Zero Risk Option available in cave rescues, the children would theoretically have had to remain inside chamber nine until the waters had subsided. But we were in the early phases of monsoon season; that meant the kids and the SEALs having to live in Tham Luang for months. Given the Thai's military dive teams were unable to swim to chamber nine and back with anything approaching consistency, the food distribution system would probably break down at some point and the kids would eventually starve, though the sanitation in the cave was going to cause all manner of serious health problems long before then. In that respect, the Zero Risk Option carried the likelihood of a 100 per cent mortality rate.

Many actions in life involve some form of risk. Crossing the road. Chopping onions. Getting on a plane. None of these processes are inherently *risky*, but to assume none of them present any potential consequences whatsoever is incredibly naïve. We might step into the road, unthinking, and walk into the path of a speeding bus. While chopping onions, our super-sharp knife might slip and cause a terrible injury. I won't go into the potential risks of flying just in case anyone reading this is aerophobic, but there are plenty of Hollywood films that depict the worst-case scenarios, should you wish to go there.

Strangely, as a society, we seem to have forgotten that everything we do in life carries risks – both big and small. When a serious car accident happens, or a gas explosion takes place, bold statements are made. *This must never be allowed to happen again.* Sometimes overzealous safety measures are installed in the aftermath. But continuing that line of thinking to its logical conclusion would see us banning cars (there were 1,580 road traffic deaths in the UK during the year ending June 2020) and cutting off domestic gas supplies in the home. Sober reality requires us to accept that those risks exist. Then it's up to us to acknowledge which threats we feel are acceptable, and then work to mitigate them as best we can.

When crossing the road, actually take the time to look as well as listen.

When chopping onions with a very sharp knife, cut along a line that's away from the body.

When settling into your plane seat, watch the safety instruction video instead of flicking through the movie menu. (That can wait for five minutes, surely?)

These are simple precautions. And rather than living in a constant state of ignorance at one end of the spectrum, and hyper-anxiety at the other, we can learn to accept the consequences of our actions. Most of all, we should forget the concept of the Zero Risk Option.

It simply doesn't exist.

LET THE SEDIMENT SETTLE

For Rick and me, the very act of doing nothing – other than checking our equipment and fleshing out our plans – was very much a proactive effort. We needed to slow down the pace of our work to ensure due diligence: nobody wanted to injure or kill another person by rushing through the eventual rescue, or through forgetting to check a vital piece of kit (which then might fail at the worst possible time). In that moment, patience and care were essential traits.

And so much had already gone wrong! We had had to rescue workers trapped inside the cave. Saman had died while operating underwater. Those mysterious 'epileptic fits' too. But the most telling example of how moving too quickly could cause problems in a crisis situation was evidenced by those Thai Navy SEALs stuck in the cave alongside the Wild Boars. Had the military not been so determined to charge in, a plan might have been executed in such a way that all four operators could have swum back to the cave entrance without any drama. Instead, their eagerness to push the mission forward created an even bigger problem.

Rushing or panicking in a crisis is something that every one of us is guilty of from time to time. For some people it happens in a moment of high emotion. They hear something that upsets them in a domestic or business disagreement, and rather than slowing down and listening to the words that are actually being spoken, they crash headlong into a defensive position, which then only intensifies the conflict. Other people are guilty of agreeing to an exciting or potentially rewarding work commitment too quickly, only to discover a few days later that they have double-booked themselves, or over committed. The cancellation process can be embarrassing, but by simply stopping to think about what was being proposed in the first place, they could have saved a whole lot of grief.

Instead, in moments when immediate action is not required, it is often best to actively *do nothing*, and it's an option I have relied upon a lot while cave diving, especially if an exploration has become a little hairy. At times, when swimming into a new chamber for example, it's very common for the world around a diver to darken. A thick, cloudy sediment – puffed up by their movements – billows about them and during those dark moments, cocooned in the murk, the simple process of establishing up from down can seem difficult. It's not unusual to feel nauseous or dizzy when the senses have been cut off from any point of reference. Unaware of where they're going, a diver can panic. They might lose their grip on the line, or bump into a rocky outcrop or wall. But an experienced individual knows that if they are able to wait calmly for just a little while – in essence, *do nothing* – the sediment washing around them will eventually settle, and their visibility and bearings will return. They can then work their way forward.

The questions everybody should ask before reacting quickly in a crisis situation are these:

1) Will my immediate reactions make things worse?

2) Or will they move me towards where I want to be?

So in diving terms, does thrashing around in the water, desperately looking for a guideline, increase an individual's chance of survival in a risky situation? *No, they'll only become more confused and increasingly distanced from the correct way forward.* Does a bickering husband, or wife benefit from always charging headlong into a passionate defence of their actions during an argument? *Not likely, they'll only inflame the dispute and leave the other person feeling frustrated and misunderstood. They should instead listen and acknowledge the words of their partner.* In a lot of crisis situations, it is often far better to simply step back and read the events swirling around, rather than worsen the situation with a poorly considered word or action.

This is a theory I had previously stress-tested during a dive into Font del Truffe – a popular flooded cave in the Lot region of France. The appeal of exploring it was obvious: Font del Truffe's water was almost always crystal clear; a scenic, but small lake provided easy access to the spectacular underwater passages beyond, via one small squeeze down a gravel bank and under an arch. Once inside, the cave consisted of fourteen flooded sections, though most divers only visited the first couple of sumps. Rarely did anyone move beyond the fourth chamber because the effort to arrive there required a complex and heavy-going trudge through a dry cave while carrying lots of bulky equipment. At the very end, in the twelfth flooded section, an intimidating squeeze known as a rift had curtailed any previous explorations.

In the same way that mountaineering expeditions are planned in different ways, so it was possible to tackle Font del Truffe in one of two varied styles. The first was to move in the expedition manner, whereby a support team helped the lead divers by load-carrying any equipment over the tunnels' dry sections. The second method was to travel light and quickly, and with limited equipment. In the mountaineering world this was known as moving *alpine-style*, and Rick and I had chosen to follow this particular model. Our aim: to swim through the twelfth chamber, into the rift and then beyond.

Further strain was caused by the logistics of what promised to be a very tricky dive. In order to streamline ourselves, we decided to remove our buoyancy devices at the start of sump twelve so as to be able to squeeze through the final rift. Neither of us wanted to get our body pinned that deep inside Font del Truffe, but this only added to the complications we could expect at depth: without our buoyancy devices, there was every chance we might become *negatively buoyant*, meaning we'd be heavy enough to almost 'bottom walk' across the cave floor. Elsewhere, to ensure that we weren't overloaded with kit throughout the journey, we both staged various cylinders and equipment along the route. That way, we could collect and drop them off as we saw necessary, changing, or adjusting our essentials while progressing in a streamlined fashion. Every piece was vital. Missing just one changeover would scupper the trip; at worst it might prove fatal.

After negotiating over 2 kilometres of diving, interspersed with crawling, walking and some desperate climbs both up and down, we surfaced into the pool before sump twelve. As I looked at the desolate high rift ahead of me, the sheer smooth walls rose up from the water and stretched vertically into the blackness as far as my lights would penetrate. I realised there was no place here to exit the water even if I wanted to. I fastened my buoyancy devices to the guideline and recalled the plan. Rick was diving into the rift first; I would wait for ten minutes and then follow. And when my moment arrived, I swam down through a complex set of right-angled fissures in the rock, diving ever deeper, twisting and turning my way into the narrow passages. My view was incredible. The rock was spectacularly white, the water exceptionally clear, and ahead I noticed several wispy, granular curlicues – spirals of silt wafted up by Rick's fins as he had pressed ahead.

The cave's depth increased until, eventually I arrived at the previous limit of exploration – the deepest part of the sump. The visibility around me had worsened and, taking a moment to assess my location, I noticed the silt on the floor. There was plenty of it and a series of marks revealed where Rick had almost crawled along the bottom, laying a yellow guideline as he advanced. It disappeared into the inky blackness ahead – *the unknown.*

I shivered. The depths had compressed my wetsuit so tightly that the material seemed plastered to my body – it felt almost paper-thin and the cold pinched at my flesh. My nerves tingled too. And having followed Rick's line, I suddenly understood why previous divers had experienced second thoughts about progressing. The passage ahead resembled a living room fireplace and I'd have to crawl in and then up, into a stone tube that was no more than 50 centimetres wide. That would have been unsettling enough for anyone suffering from the slightest tremors of claustrophobia. However, I was at a depth of 30 metres, a place where every sense became intensified. My head felt woozy from the narcosis of breathing from a rebreather, too, and given I was several kilometres from the surface, this was no place to get stuck. I would die, trapping Rick in the tunnels ahead – unless he was able to shift my corpse on the way out.

Taking a moment to settle I recalled a practised mantra for situations such as this: *I'm psychologically ready. I can do it. Stay calm.* Then I turned off my rebreather, hanging it parallel to my side in a line, so as to minimise my body profile. *In, out. In, out.* I felt my breath rising and falling through the regulator connected to my bailout cylinder*. At this depth I knew I had around a minute to spare, but beyond that, I risked using up too much gas and I would need every litre of it to exit Font del Truffe safely. My heart pounded as I peered into the submerged chimney.

Here we go.

The clock was ticking; this was no place to hang about, and I was forced to tackle the squeeze like a Victorian chimney sweep. Bending backwards unnaturally, I was able to wriggle inside, but only just, and without my buoyancy device I felt desperately heavy. Each pull and lift took me a little higher into the narrow channel. Every advance brought relief. My wetsuit was loosening as the water pressure released its grip, and slowly I became more buoyant. I started to float upwards until, at 20 metres, the rift widened enough for me to swing my rebreather onto my chest. I could draw on my regular gas supply once more. Edging my way out of the shoulder-width tube and into an air space, I found Rick, beaming at me. We had extended the known limits of Font del Truffe.

And then the trouble began.

It was now my turn to lead, and having set our guideline through a beautiful, clean-washed passage to reach another air space, we had decided to turn around. Getting back would require us to negotiate the chimney once more, though at least this time we could allow gravity to do its work. Shifting my rebreather to one side, I plunged down the chute like a stone.

---

* Bailout cylinders are normally used when a diver's primary breathing apparatus fails, which in this case was the rebreather. In Font del Truffe we had decided to use our bailout cylinders on the way into the chimney to become as streamlined as possible, but this was considered unorthodox because doing so used up precious gas normally reserved for an emergency exit.

bedside manner was being put to the test too: through a translator we explained what was about to take place, before reassuring and cajoling our test subjects as we pulled them under the water. At certain points I asked that they try to keep as still as possible, and having suggested that any feeling of fear, or discomfort should be communicated by a squeeze of the hand, I soon realised there were actually more complications to consider during a rehearsal than there would be inside Tham Luang. For starters we were planning on sedating the Wild Boars, so they weren't likely to wriggle or thrash underwater. There also wouldn't be a viewing gallery of stony-faced spectators inside chamber nine.

Eventually, Rick, Jason, Chris and I went to work. And as the large crowd looked on nervously, our volunteers were transported this way and that, the handles attached to their backs holding firm. In the worst-case scenario drill, where I imagined losing hold of a kid, it was possible to relocate him by pulling the lanyard attached to the boy's harness. Elsewhere, the lead weight at the front of our 'casualty's' buoyancy device prevented him from rolling in the water. Our procedure had stood up to scrutiny, and when I eventually pulled away my face mask and looked around the swimming pool, the crowd was dispersing. The doom-laden vibe had passed. Even the gathered medics, all of them on tenterhooks at the start of the session, were now staring at their phones absentmindedly. By the looks of it, we had brought the authorities around to our line of thinking.

We were on to something.

Kidding myself into believing that the hard yards had been completed was a dangerous move, though. I recognised that the challenges ahead were still undeniably difficult, and dangerous, but there was reassurance in the fact that our instincts had been correct. *The Inert Package Plan* was feasible. After another hour or so underwater, we could see that both the British and Euro teams were very much up to the task. Any diver that might have felt uncertain or rusty when negotiating some of the finer details of the operation – such as how best to move the kids underwater, or when to reassure them – was given the opportunity to practise the subtle nuances of their role. Rick and I looked on, our confidence rising. The plan to evacuate four boys a day was coming together.

This familiarisation process was turbocharged later that day. A 3D version of Rick's notorious A2 whiteboard had been constructed at the dive base as part of a process the American Air Force referred to as a *Rehearsal Of Concept* (ROC) drill. A large, green fence had been placed around the area to shield us from the press and a length of rope detailing the guideline had been laid across the ground, linking our 'dummy' starting point at dive base to the kids waiting in chamber nine. All sorts of furniture was being used as signposts across the route, sometimes literally. Plastic chairs signified various air chambers within the caverns, while colour-coded, half-litre water bottles represented the type of assets that were set to be staged throughout Tham Luang, such as oxygen cylinders. Laminated sheets of A4 paper dangled from the line like bunting, each one denoting a different area of the cave.

With such a setup it was possible to perform a walkthrough of the operation, but we must have looked an odd bunch. In full view of each other, the divers moved one by one around the line in quick order towards the Wild Boars (another collection of plastic bottles). On cue, various support rescuers assumed their positions by the plastic chairs to facilitate cylinder changeovers.

Bumps and misunderstandings happened along the way; there was some confusion over where various air pockets were actually located. When I looked up, I noticed that the same stern faces that had briefly watched on the sidelines of the pool were now scrutinising us from the shadows. But after several dry runs and debates, collisions and readjustments, all performed with the assistance of the US Air Force, we were able to repeat the sequence without error. A clear timetable of action was established, as was the running order of divers for each day.

During this time, rehearsals of another type were taking place in the cave. The dry passages that led from chamber three to the entrance had been rigged by a team of Thai engineers and Navy SEALs with ziplines designed to speed the boys' evacuation. These ropeways were tested using a stretcher loaded with a volunteer. (It hung horizontally below the zipline as the boy would.) This evacuation exercise from dive base was performed several times, and during a final dry run the smallest female member of the US Air Force team, Airman First Class Haley Moulton had agreed to be the casualty. The thinking was that she would be much closer in size to the boys and immediately a problem presented itself as she almost slipped through the bottom stretcher, which led to a rethink on the tension required for the securing straps. Another potential issue had been ironed out through practice.

I soon felt very appreciative of our two, slightly unorthodox rehearsal sessions. If anybody had been under any illusions as to what was expected of us, the realities of our workload and responsibilities were now crystal clear. The effort had also sharpened our understanding of process, though just as importantly, it looked to have convinced the authorities of our abilities too.

There's little doubt our techniques had been viewed with a healthy dollop of scepticism at first, and without that level of preparation, plus one or two demonstrations of competence, there's every chance the mission would have been canned. Instead, we were readying ourselves for what would ultimately prove to be the most audacious rescue job of our lives.

■ ■ ■

That night, before going to bed, I spent a little time visualising the worst-case scenario: *one of the boys I'd been moving had stopped breathing*. When I imagined looking into the face mask, I visualised his eyes, magnified through the water, all glassy and lifeless; they were staring right through me. *He was gone.* I tried to experience the inevitable emotions in advance – the sense of shock; the pain of tragedy; the sensations as a wave of guilt, anger, and anxiety washed over me. Some people might have considered my actions to be a form of catastrophising, an invited self-fulfilling prophecy, or even an act of masochism that was setting me up for long-term failure. In reality, a psychological drill of this kind had long acted as a positive form of self-defence. I wanted to be ready should one of the boys die under my care during the mission, and by repeating this exercise, building up my emotional responses in advance and putting them into training, I felt ready for the horrors that might drift my way. I was filing away more plans in the library, just in case.

This was a technique I'd employed during our first few days in Tham Luang, as we'd searched for the boys. During those stormy nights, the rain hammering at the corrugated iron roof of our room, I'd imagined swimming into a chamber filled with thirteen dead bodies. They swayed and spun in the water like discarded plastic bags. I saw those same, grisly movements again on the eve of the extraction, only this time I was visualising a moment in which I'd entered a sump with a living child and exited with a corpse.

How would I continue in such an event? God, the thought of it felt desperate. Even though someone had died on me, I'd still need to get to the entrance of the cave in order to save myself, and by extension another Wild Boar the next day. We'd been instructed to bring the boys all the way out, even if they'd died in transit, but that carried a mortal risk for everyone involved. *Was it really worth dying while attempting to bring a dead person to the surface?* I was prepared to risk my life for a breathing child, no question. If I found myself in a tight spot, and it seemed feasible to do so, I was OK with being marooned in an air chamber with whichever Wild Boar I was trying to save. However, I wasn't going to kill myself by trying to bring through a boy who had already passed away. That night, I imagined myself surfacing with a dead child at dive base and absorbed the sense of shame and failure I would feel in the aftermath. My determination to avoid that situation at all costs intensified further.

There was also the fear that I might somehow lose a living boy in the murk. The lanyards and handles affixed to the kids had been designed to prevent such an incident, but there was still the slightest chance that an equipment malfunction *could* happen. In much the same way that a parachute sometimes fails from time to time, the chances were admittedly slim, but they were there nevertheless. I browsed the Library of Plans for a solution: in such an unlikely event, I decided the smartest play would be search for the child as long as I had the air to swim us both to safety – whether that was inside the cave or dive base. Beyond that, there was really no point exhausting my entire air supply only to find the kid as my last breath expired. In that situation, both of us would have died shortly afterwards.

While this was an undeniably morbid train of thought, I felt morally comfortable with the choices I might have to make during the rescue. There would be little time to think or theorise if ever those imagined situations became a reality, but with my responses figured out in advance I'd be able to operate more effectively. Visualisation, I knew, was a powerful motivator and I was using it keenly, hoping it might push me away from failure. I felt an indescribably strong determination that, whatever the coming rescue held for the others, I would not make a mistake; that I would ensure *my* children at least would survive.

Meanwhile there was also the unnerving business of sedation to consider. Harry had agreed to administer the ketamine from inside the cave, but his work stopped with the injections, and in doing so he was already putting his medical career on the line. But no matter how difficult the journey out with the boys proved, I wouldn't have swapped places with him for anything – I hated the thought of sedating those kids, even though there was no other option.

Unfortunately, I'd have to involve myself in the process from time to time. Given the journey from chamber nine to dive base was taking us around four hours, Harry's initial dose of sedative was almost certain to wear off before the boys in transit had been moved to safety. They would begin to stir in very distressing circumstances. This meant everyone involved would have to be prepared to administer further, top-up doses and so all the divers needed a training session on the intricacies of intramuscular injections. When we arrived for our briefing, Harry had laid out an intimidating line of syringes for us to use.

As a trained first aider with around twelve years of experience at the time, I was fairly familiar with some of the more squeamish aspects of delivering an injection – in theory anyway. During a number of courses, the practice of giving an intramuscular jab had been explained to me, in case I had to use one during a cave rescue. But rather than performing the injection on a real, live person, I remember we'd rehearsed on an orange. The reasons for this were fairly obvious at the time: an orange has a slightly tougher, exterior skin with a pulpy 'flesh' underneath, which feels similar to a human, and during those first-aid programmes, I'd made light of the situation by drawing a smiley face on the fruit with a marker pen. When faced with the prospect of administering a shot of ketamine to a semi-conscious boy in Tham Luang, the jokes quickly evaporated.

Everyone was uncomfortable. As Harry presented a bare essentials course on delivering the shots, I was able to treat the lessons as a refresher exercise. For some of the others, it must have felt terrifyingly new. Our anxieties were heightened further by the fact that all we had to practise on were plastic water bottles. There were no smiley oranges in sight.

'What does it feel like when injecting a person for the very first time, Harry?' I asked, my needle slipping into the plastic.

'Oh, well the first time you do it, you'll probably shit yourself,' he said, smiling. 'But once you've got the first one done, you'll be as right as rain.'

I trusted Harry's opinion. During the brief time we'd worked together, a bond had undoubtedly grown between us – he, too, felt an incredible sense of ownership for rescuing the Wild Boars. His broad Australian accent and down-to-earth demeanour also helped to add a little levity to the occasion, and by the end of the session everybody had been handed a waterproof kit bag containing syringes, needles and ketamine, with doses labelled *Big Kid* and *Small Kid*. (Though thankfully, these were changed to one-size-fits-all, medium doses after day one.) We were now staring down the barrel of a risk-loaded rescue.

VISUALISATION: PROCESS AND PAIN

A lot has been written about the process of visualisation, especially within fields where a focus on the desired, winner-takes-all result is vital. (Think sport, business, or endurance events.) In such cases, people are encouraged to keep their eye on the prize, or to imagine a lap of victory, in an approach that is not dissimilar to a donkey being led along by a carrot dangling from the end of a stick. Sure, it's a style of inspiration that works for some. The autobiographies of sports stars, adventurers and business leaders are full of moments of crippling doubt where some imagined spoils of success have then driven them on. But I have found that this approach really doesn't work for me. From what I've heard, I am not alone in thinking this way, not least because at some level you actually have to *believe* that you can be successful. Focusing on wishy-washy moments of glory that might not actually come to anything seems to me like a waste of mental calories.

To begin with, I experience a fair amount of imposter syndrome, as a lot of people do. The very act of writing this book has caused me to feel fraudulent at times, and somewhat exposed. As a consequence, I tend to squirm a little at any event where I am the centre of attention, so picturing the rewards of success or a moment of glory as a motivating device doesn't work. I don't want to imagine myself standing in front of a cheering audience with a gold medal around my neck. The thought of an applauding crowd of peers as I collect an *Employee of the Year Award* leaves me cold. I'd much prefer that my efforts were driven by the joy of process and technique rather than any potential rewards or accolades.

I have also found that focusing on nothing more than the end game can be joyless and rather counter-productive – simply visualising future moments of success and satisfaction can create a false sense of security, while the reality of what is actually required to succeed remains in the psychological shadows. Instead, I tend to focus my attentions on the actions and techniques required to reach that successful outcome. Then I'll imagine them in detail, whether they're positive or negative. Having visualised what needs to be done and how, I'm ready to negotiate the practical stages as and when they arrive for real.

For instance, before a dive, I will picture myself in a positive place. I'll feel myself moving through the water: I can see currents roiling around me, my hand on the line, the waft of my fins as I glide forward. From the comfort of my armchair, I am taking a positive and low-impact training session, where all the skills I might need to reach my target are committed to memory. Professional golfers are understandably obsessed with the concept of process and think in much the same way. Before every shot, they'll stand behind the ball and create the perfect swing in their mind. Having imagined the sweet sensation as club and ball connect, their shot then arcs upwards into the air and surges towards its intended target, landing softly on the green and rolling steadily towards the hole.

This technique works well in all manner of situations. A case in point: when imagining an important exam, such as a driving test, it's more helpful to visualise the techniques required to perform the perfect three-point turn, or a successful parallel parking manoeuvre, than to imagine the examiner as they congratulate you on your success at the end. Likewise, diets, or nutrition plans can fail psychologically when people look past the rituals required to succeed. Instead, they constantly dream of eating chocolate at the finish line (driving the very behaviour they want to avoid). However, by training their attention on new cooking skills, or the interest of creating a menu of delicious and nutritionally rewarding dinners, it's possible to make the process more enjoyable and draw the desired result into reality more effectively.

In a complicated diving exploration, I'll often visualise the processes in play, such as exactly where I have to stage, or switch various gas cylinders. In each case, I'll see myself executing the task perfectly. Rebreathers, for example, demand great respect. In open water there is a lot to consider when using one, and plenty can go wrong, but deep underground, divers are usually much further from home. (And by home, I mean safety.) Rebreathers contain chemicals that absorb exhaled carbon dioxide. When these chemicals are exhausted, or the diver breathes too quickly, the CO^2 level in the system increases in a runaway effect that can cause the user to pant. This creates anxiety, which, in turn, forces a diver to breathe even harder, until eventually they fall unconscious. Unable to swap mouthpieces, they will inevitably drown.

This horrific situation can be avoided by changing to a safe or bailout form of gas in advance, and I have often prepared for such a worst-case scenario in my recurring visualisations. I imagine vividly the uncontrollable panting and a growing sense of anxiety. I try to feel the vice-like clutch of fear around my throat and a desperate desire to swap regulators, even though I am unable to remove the rebreather mouthpiece. On hundreds of occasions I've even visualised wrestling with the very human urge to keep panting, while reaching for an imaginary spare regulator hanging round my neck. In my mind I have then pressed the purge button*, creating a pillow of air beneath my face. The bad mouthpiece is then thrown away as I choke and splutter, safely, into the new regulator.

It's also important to visualise and psychologically rehearse, for scenarios that we have grown accustomed to handling with ease. Often it's all too easy to forget the pain endured during our past successes because the brain has a tremendous capacity for gifting us with rose-tinted spectacles. A good example would be the 100-mile race, or ultra-marathon, where the completion rate for people on their second run is often lower than those runners striving to complete an ultra-marathon for the very first time.

The reason for this is very simple: when taking on such a gruelling challenge, first-timers arrive with a readied state of mind. They know the experience is set to be intense; there is a very good chance they might collapse way before the finishing line, and so they do everything they can in training to avoid failure. They run right; they eat right; they prepare right. On the day of the race, they use every trick in the book to locate extra

---

* The purge button, which is positioned on the second stage of a regulator, causes air to rush from the device. This is normally used to clear water in the mouthpiece so a diver can breathe safely from it again.

sources of motivation, internal and external, and their friends and family will line the course and shout words of encouragement. *There's a novelty factor.*

Eventually, after crossing the line, a sense of achievement kicks in. They think, '*I did it*,' but for many people it's easy to forget how they were pushed to the edges of their capacity. Complacency strikes. (And I know all about this, having competed in a number of ultra-marathons.) When the time arrives to train for a second race, they forget the intense pain of running incredibly long distances – and they quit. Or they lose sight of just how difficult a race of that kind can be – and skip training. Having thought only of the fact that they completed the test last time around, the gruelling psychological effort required to succeed is blocked out – and they fail.

What I am suggesting is quite the opposite. *We should remember the pain.* In much the same way a successful football manager might tell his team to forget the last cup final win, or any glories from the previous season – because another very different campaign is about to begin – so the ultra-marathon runner should put aside the glow of completion when committing to a new race. Rather than thinking, 'I'm an ultra-marathon runner now, I can do it,' they might do better to recall those moments when failure seemed likely. They should picture the times when, 70 miles into the last attempt, they dropped to their hands and knees in agony and puked their guts up. Or staggered towards the finish, their feet bleeding. These painful moments are strong psychological markers, as are the intervals during a race when the mind wanders to its darkest places.

Then, having relived all that discomfort and effort before

their training programme begins, they can recall how they were able to summon the strength to succeed when difficulties arose last time around:

I got through this before. I know how it feels . . .

. . . And I can do it again.

The agony won't come as shock that way. The emotional distress is expected. And the gruelling effort required for running 100 miles arrives as no real surprise.

REHEARSE. THEN REPEAT: THE CHECKLIST

- Understand your plan. Practise, practise, practise.

- Visualise your feelings. Rehearse your reactions.

- Recall the pain of success. Acknowledge the effort required.

LESSON #12

MAKE SUCCESS A HABIT

In any walk of life it's important we see our commitments through to the end and then turn the process of completion into a habit. It's one of the reasons why certain business figures rise at 5 a.m. and then stay up until midnight – they are keenly focused on advancing their company, or project, and they want to accomplish again and again, over and over. While I'm not advocating such an unhealthy sleeping routine, there are rituals that we can adapt from individuals of this kind. Wanting to succeed, disliking the thought of failure, and sticking resolutely to a challenge are key traits we can all throw into our toolbox, because they're applicable to every aspect of our day to day life – at work, in the gym, even at home. As I was to discover, they would function just as well in Tham Luang where I exhausted every last reserve of strength to see the rescue through . . .

DAY THIRTEEN
SUNDAY 8 JULY 2018

The mood was up. The rescue team was raring to go, but I simply couldn't understand the rush of optimism that was bouncing about the place. According to weather forecasts, more rainstorms were on the way, which meant the clock was ticking. I found it impossible to shake the dreadful feeling that we were engaged in a race against time, and that in our eagerness to save thirteen people we might just kill them all. Major 'Charlie' Charles Hodges, the US Mission Commander for the 353rd Special Operations Unit of the Air Force sensed my concern. He stepped up with a vaguely reassuring pep talk.

'John, without your help, those kids are as good as dead anyway,' he said.

While I appreciated his logic, I worried how a tragedy or death under my watch might affect me emotionally over the coming hours and days, and even in the long term. I worked to harden my resolve with a private pep talk of my own:

Yeah, the process might be risky. Some of the kids might not survive, but the boys I'm caring for absolutely will make it through.

Steadying my inner conviction was a vital first step. With a start time of 10 a.m. confirmed, there was no room for doubt and even less room for confusion. Rick, Jason and Chris, plus our support divers, gathered together and talked through the order of events once more.

Three days.

Four boys are coming out on day one; another four on day two; then four on the final day, plus the coach.

Jason goes in first and swims his Wild Boar to dive base in chamber three.

Then John.

Next up is Chris. Rick will wait in chamber eight and head in last with any medical notes for Harry on how the sedations are working out. With the help of Craig, he can assess whether the dosages are too big, too small or spot on.

This final detail was important. We hoped to fine-tune our experimental (and very worrying) medical procedures as quickly as possible if we were to extract all the Wild Boars before another storm struck. Everybody knew what they were doing; when the moment to swim towards chamber nine arrived, there was nothing in the way of fanfare. Jason dropped into the waters at dive base and then disappeared from view.

'Oh fuck,' I thought. *'Me next . . .'*

The journey to the Wild Boars' temporary home was as gruelling as ever. Handily, the cave appeared to be in a more agreeable mood and the waters had lowered further, but I was in no doubt that an incoming weather system might increase their ferocity almost immediately. Having arrived at chamber nine in one piece, it was a relief to see that the operation had taken on a life of its own. So far, events were running exactly as planned. Four boys were in varying stages of preparation, but I had no idea who was coming out first and how the decision had been arrived at. Harry had left the organisation of a timetable up to the Wild Boars themselves and a short meeting had taken place on the bank. A departure list was prepared.

From what I could tell, Coach Ek had decided that those from the neighbourhood of Ban San Wiang Hom should be the first out. They lived the farthest away, after all, and therefore imagined they would have the longest cycle ride home for food. That meant Note, Tern, Nick and Night were coming out first. It was a very sweet suggestion of Ek's, but also a telling sign that none of the stranded kids, or their responsible adult, had the faintest clue as to the emergency services, military personnel and international media ranged outside the cave. Jason had already dressed Note and taken him for sedation. Assisted by Harry, the first unconscious passenger was placed into the water; the boy's buoyancy jacket and full-face mask were securely fastened. There was no turning back for him now.

When I looked around, the SEALs were helping two more boys on the bank as they wriggled into their wetsuits. Each wore a neoprene hood packed with foam padding to further protect their heads. (Wearing a caving helmet was impossible because the boys' diving masks covered the entire face.) But the most chilling detail was the plastic cable ties that had been wrapped around the wrist of each passenger – the kind you might see attached to prisoners in a war film, or police drama. Though they weren't yet snapped together, the boys' arms had to be bound behind their backs with a karabiner once the sedation had kicked in, and while this might have seemed inhumane, the restraints were in place so that the passenger's arms and hands would stay secure during the journey. Dangling free, their limbs might become caught, or even snap against a rock. Worse, if the ketamine was to wear off while one of the boys was still underwater, he might tear at his face mask in a sudden panic. The Wild Boars giggled as they watched their mates being dressed for what would be an incredibly dangerous journey. *It was like a game to them.*

Medically, our plan was running smoothly. Each boy had been given a Xanax tranquilliser prior to being sedated. That way he would be suitably relaxed for his ketamine injection fifteen minutes later. Harry was now on the bank, perched some way in the water, the next passenger sitting upon his knee. *My passenger.* A syringe was stuck into both legs, straight through the wetsuit – one shot of ketamine as a sedative; the other a shot of atropine, which was often administered to dry up a patient's saliva during surgical procedures. While drowning in floodwater was the biggest threat to the boys in Tham Luang, we feared they could just as easily choke on their own saliva. Every dose was calculated through educated guesswork. Harry sized up his patients expertly and judged their shot based on size and weight, taking into account possible dehydration and malnutrition.

The boy seemed relaxed in his company. Having spent a number of years working as an anaesthetist, Harry had clearly built up a reassuring bedside manner, and whenever one of the kids looked up nervously, he asked him about football, or sport. Because of his Aussie accent, Harry's jokes were landing well.

'You've got John taking you out,' he said.

John? The boy looked confused.

'Yes. *Lucky you!* He's the best one . . .' continued Harry.

There was a nervous smile.

Over the coming days, Harry would repeat the same trick for every boy, with Jason, Rick and Chris being given the same pseudo-praise. His chatty demeanour helped to put the Wild Boars at ease, though it probably also went some way to keeping his own stresses under control. We were all experiencing them.

I watched from the sidelines as the ketamine did its work. The passenger's eyes glazed, and then drooped, before closing over. *He was out cold.*

'He's all yours, John,' said Harry, supporting the boy as we moved him into the water.

The mask was placed over his face. It covered his eyes, nose, mouth and chin like a Perspex bubble. The passenger's head was immediately airtight; the built-in regulator provided the oxygen he needed to breathe, and he was able to inhale freely from the attached cylinder. Then came the most uncomfortable safety check of all: carefully, I pushed the kid's face underwater for several seconds, checking for any leaks or cracks in the mask seal. The very act felt horrific, and I hated it.

My anxiety was rising now. Peering down at the passenger's lifeless body, I noticed he had stopped breathing and the tell-tale signs of a functioning air cylinder, those tiny bubbles that rose through the water in ribbons, were nowhere to be seen. Maybe the cold water had shocked his system? Or perhaps it had something to do with the ketamine? I really didn't know. Trying to remain calm I pressed the purge button on his regulator in an attempt to force more oxygen into his lungs. *Nothing.* I pressed again. *Still no response.*

'Oh no,' I thought looking up at Harry nervously. 'This is not good.'

Finally, after a few seconds, the boy seemed to relax. I spotted the first curlicue of air in the water and puffed out a sigh of relief. He was exhaling.

It's OK . . .

. . . Now for the tricky bit.

There was no backing out now, though I desperately wanted to. The thought of swimming for over 1.5 kilometres through churning water and scrambling over rocky terrain – somehow without killing the child in my care – filled me with dread. I strapped the air cylinder to the passenger's chest and positioned him face down in the water once more; his buoyancy jacket was holding him on the surface. I then attached the cargo to my harness with a lanyard so he wouldn't float away into the dark at any point. My safety checks complete, I swam towards the tunnels, pushing and pulling the lifeless body along with me.

I felt stressed. My stomach knotted; the muscles around my Adam's apple had constricted a little. *Was I experiencing stage fright?* Everything was moving so fast and yet my subconscious was telling me to slow down, or at least to maintain some form of emotional control. *But how?* The rescue had taken on a momentum all of its own, and in double-quick time, so there was no room for a time-out, or some moment of silent contemplation. And then a thought struck me. *I didn't know which boy I was swimming with.* Where that sudden urge to identify who I was rescuing had come from, I'm not entirely sure, because previously it had felt important to protect the other divers from becoming too attached to the kids as they swam into chamber nine with food, supplies or notes. I hadn't got to know the kids by their names but I wanted to remind myself that the package I was about to transport, while being very much inert, was a human being, *and just a kid.* More importantly, he was also a son, a friend and maybe even a brother to any number of people waiting anxiously beyond the cave.

I shouted back to Chris on the bank.

'What's his name?'

But Chris didn't know, and it was too late to lean down and ask. The poor kid had already been sedated. I would have to do without.

I learned later, after the first day of rescues, that my passenger was Tern. He was slight of build and I was glad to be transporting one of the smaller boys – physically it would make my work a little easier. Whenever I had visited the Wild Boars in chamber nine, Tern had always appeared full of life, despite being stuck in a gloomy cave with no light, no comforts and not much in the way of decent food. I remembered his big smile.

As we moved further and further away from the bank and the watching boys, a funny thing happened. My anxiety was instantly outweighed by a feeling of loneliness, one I hadn't experienced during the operation so far. Face down in the water I could see the murk shifting and shimmering as sediment flows churned this way and that. I heard the sound of percolating air bubbles and felt the wash of water in my ears. But none of those experiences were new or unusual. Nor was the weight of Tern's lifeless body as I carried him alongside me – the bags of supplies I had transported into the Wild Boars previously had been just as heavy.

What *was* different this time around was the burden of responsibility – and it felt crushing. Tern's survival was all on me; I was beyond the reach of Harry and medical help, and that was a massive psychological weight to carry. I didn't feel entirely comfortable about it, either. Having glanced down, the flesh of Tern's palms, now bound together behind his back, suddenly seemed so very pale in the glare of my torchlight, his soles too. It reminded me of just how vulnerable the boy was in the water. I did my best not to scrape his feet along the bottom of the cave, though my main concern was to protect the seal of his face mask. If a head cracked against the roof at any point, it had to be my head. If a face mask were to dislodge in the currents, it would have to be my face mask. Keeping the boy breathing was my top priority.

The feeling of isolation was so powerful that I felt slightly envious of Tern's sedated state. A Xanax would have gone some way to smoothing off the ragged emotional edges. It also might have helped to referee the strange wrestling match taking place inside my head. Part of me very much accepted the realities of our situation; I understood that it was my job to get three boys out of the Tham Luang caves over the next few days, and that I had been given the task, alongside Rick, Jason and Chris, because we were the divers best placed to execute the mission.

'It's right that I'm doing this,' I told myself. *'Who else could do it?'*

But experience also made me keenly aware of the consequences were I to make a mistake at any point. Which is probably why the early symptoms of imposter syndrome were beginning to emerge.

'I don't want to be here,' I thought. *'I want to be out of it.'*

I attempted to pump the brakes on what was fast becoming a runaway train of negative thoughts, and kicked forward.

Do the job . . . And do it well.

The first sump of our fraught journey together was coming into view. Releasing a little air from Tern's buoyancy jacket, I pushed him forward into the deeper waters. There was zero resistance. It was like moving a corpse, and with one hand on the line, I submerged him into the black, his body beneath mine. I had chosen to cradle the passenger's head beneath my chin – *I had to protect him from the rocky knuckles above* – and we progressed for around twenty minutes. At intervals I peered down to check the boy was still breathing by counting the time between his exhalations. Given his position, a small stream of bubbles appeared in front of my face mask with every gasp of air; they really were the only sign of life. And worryingly, the intervals between breaths were undoubtedly lengthening; time seemed to be slowing. Every now and then, I feared that Tern's lungs might have stopped working altogether. Unable to remove his mask, I'd press at the purge button on his regulator, hoping to force a little oxygen into his chest, my stress spiking until the tell-tale bubbles drifted past my face once more.

Tension was building. More than anything, I wanted to avoid the distressing exchanges of condolence that would have to take place if he died. The idea of being introduced to Tern's parents – had he stopped breathing under my care – and then having to express my sorrow and regret would have been too painful to bear. *I'm so sorry for your loss.* Just the thought of saying those words left me feeling desolate, and my every ounce of strength was going to be needed to ensure it didn't happen. I pushed him even further into the deep and pressed on.

■ ■ ■

There was a shape in the water ahead.

As it moved closer, the shadowy silhouette of a diver came into view and I soon recognised the face mask. *It was Rick!* But there was no time to stop and wave a cheery hello or communicate further. Instead, we passed on the line in a well-rehearsed move, shifting our hands around each other without once losing contact with the rope. As he crossed, Rick flashed me the OK sign and peered down at Tern's lifeless body. Then I noticed the confused look on his face. Apparently, Rick had assumed, wrongly, that I would wait in chamber nine until his arrival, especially as he was in possession of some important medical feedback on the state of the first boy. But our wires had been crossed and once Harry had sedated Tern, I was committed. As we parted, I knew that Rick's appearance was confirmation that Jason had made it to the first dry stretch of the rescue. *But had the kid survived, too?* Rick's expression made it impossible to tell.

Things were changing ahead of me. The water was becoming a little clearer. And as I reached forward, I noticed that the blue guideline was coming to an end and had been knotted to a thick, red climbing rope, which meant we were approaching the first dry section of the trip, the swirl cavern of chamber eight. If all went to plan, Craig Challen and Claus from the Euro team would be waiting to assist us over the rocks and into the next sump. It would also give us an opportunity to check on Tern's breathing and to make sure he wasn't regaining consciousness.

The floor was changing below me. Water gave way to sand; sand gave way to cobbles and gravel, until, eventually, I was able to float Tern to one side. The passage was low and wide, and there was very little room above – I needed to feel my way forward so as not to smash the boy's face into the rising gravel shelf. *But I was fast running out of hands!* One gripped the line, the other held on to the boy, but knowing that Tern's body couldn't drift away, I released my hold on the line, reaching ahead until I was able to feel the arch that would lead us to where Claus and Craig were supposed to be waiting with a stretcher.

But Craig wasn't there. There was no sign of Claus either. I looked this way and that, my torch beaming about the cavern, but we were still terrifyingly alone. I shouted out. *Had Craig and Claus got lost? Or worse, had Jason's boy been injured or drowned?* But there was no time for speculation; I had to heave Tern from the water. I carefully shifted his body on to the shingle beach before resting him in the recovery position, and removed his mask. *Please be breathing.* I tilted his head back, and leant close, listening for some small indication of life. Finally, it was possible to feel a faint and shallow sigh on my cheek. Tern was still alive, *thank heavens.* And then I heard the crunch of footsteps behind me. Craig had finally showed.

'All good?' he said, looking down at Tern.

I nodded. 'I think so. He's still breathing. *Where's Claus?'*

Craig shrugged and set to work on Tern as I lugged my equipment towards the next sump. By all accounts, the first dive was going well. Craig had just helped Jason on his way and Note seemed to be in once piece. Fretfully, I watched the medical assessment taking place, feeling amazed that a full-time vet, who was more versed in caring for sick household pets than children, could appear so confident and at ease when assessing a heavily sedated boy in a cave. Having become certain that Tern was fine, we manhandled him towards the next dive pool. I grabbed his hands; Craig held his feet, and we took care not to bump him on any rocks or sharp outcrops.

Suddenly there was a noise. Claus had finally arrived with the stretcher.

'Where the fuck have you been?' I shouted, my patience snapping.

Claus mumbled an excuse. I apologised and we settled down to business – I had given Claus an unfairly hard time, but he had been unsure of where to meet us, and I wasn't in the mood for excuses. I was emotionally and physically strained; my patience was frayed, and our circumstances seemed incredibly trying. This was no time for tardiness, but there was very little room for a dispute, either. I bit my tongue as the three of us loaded Tern onto the stretcher and moved him to the next diving section. Aware that the clock was ticking, I sealed the boy's mask tightly and pressed ahead. Moments later, we were submerged and moving purposefully. The world was dark once more; the only indication of life from my passenger was the occasional plume of air from his regulator mask; the only sound the muffled gurgle of bubbles as I exhaled. Loneliness had returned.

At that point, I had been swimming in and out of the cave for around ten days. The caverns and tunnels at the farthest end of Tham Luang, where the boys had been stranded, felt more familiar than ones we had repeatedly explored during the early phases of our search operation. As the guidelines changed colour ahead of me, I began recognising various ropes from my second week of diving in Thailand. We were making real progress and I was able to count down the landmarks and features around us: the body boards pinned to the roof of the cave; a length of black rope here, a stalagmite there. *We were making good progress.*

Though there were still two hours to go, some rush of excitement would have been excusable. No one would have blamed me for wanting to increase my urgency in getting Tern out of the water. However, I knew that Jason wasn't too far ahead, the last thing I wanted was to swim into a huge cloud of sediment or detritus wafted up by his fins. I had also envisioned a situation where we both arrived in the next air space at exactly the same time. With the support divers' attempting to switch two set of cylinders simultaneously, there was every chance that some terrible mistake might happen. Having come so far with Tern, the last thing I wanted was for a flash of impatience to result in an accident. I slowed my momentum and maintained a steady pace, eventually arriving in chamber six, where Erik Brown and Ivan Karadzic were waiting.

When putting together the *Inert Package Plan,* we had decided that this point in the rescue would provide each lead diver with a few minutes of rest. And while I was certainly exhausted, the idea of relinquishing responsibility for Tern, even for the briefest of moments, felt wrong. He was *my* passenger, *my* responsibility. We had come so far together, and I felt desperately protective. The thought of someone else moving him into the next stretch of water, out of my reach, was unimaginable. *Was I a control freak?* At that moment, yes – 100 per cent. I swapped out my depleted air cylinder for a full tank and carried Tern onwards into what was an open canal, swimming us towards chambers five and four. The boy, amazingly, was still sleeping peacefully.

We were nearly home. And nothing bad was going to happen on my watch.

I felt fiercely determined about that.

■ ■ ■

I could feel the current behind me now. I used it to propel us gently towards chambers five and four – some of the toughest sections of Tham Luang. At this point, the line funnelled through complicated squeezes and around rock formations as the visibility deteriorated further. Smashing into a rock with a spine-cracking bang was scary enough when travelling solo, but with an unconscious boy cradled in my arms, the associated risks had increased considerably. I feared that if I was forced to one side while wriggling through a gap in the rock, I might accidentally knock Tern's head on a limestone wall or dislodge his mask at a point where I was ten or twenty minutes away from the nearest air space. The visibility in this part of Tham Luang was also next to zero, the sediment obscuring it the result of the countless dives into this section of the cave throughout the week. Losing my grip on the line at any point would prove nightmarish and I might never rediscover it. The stakes had been raised considerably.

Even in the dark, I knew of the dangers lurking nearby. The left wall was scarred with a jagged stalactite formation and I reached out for the toothy surface, knowing it was an early sign of the struggle to come: just ahead, the tunnels pinched in, and though I was capable of pulling Tern through relatively unscathed, a series of dead, plastic glow sticks, set by divers during the rescue effort's first few days, still dangled from the guideline like oversized clothes pegs. Each one made for an unwelcome obstacle as I twisted this way and that, forced forward by the thrumming current.

My heart pounded. Though I couldn't see anything ahead of me, I knew that the safest way when negotiating this tricky stretch of terrain was to swim to the roof of the cave. Once above the guideline, it would be possible for me to feed Tern through a hole in the rock wall ahead. As my lights reflected uselessly in the heavy brown silt, I wasn't able to see it, but I knew roughly where it should be, and by feeling my way along the stalactites and outcrops I reached towards the gap. Every grab was painful. Throughout these ten days in the caves, my hands had been cut and scraped to a pulp. I hadn't worn any gloves during my dives so far – the water was warm-*ish*, and in the dark I had gained a more telling feel on the rock without them as I tried to read the walls like Braille. But a series of lacerations on my knuckles had left my flesh raw. The wounds had become pulpy and infected from the dirty water, and I was now paying the painful price.

I found the hole – *finally*. The time had come for the hard work to start. Warily, I pushed Tern ahead, careful not to catch his mask on any stalactites, and having nudged his body forwards, I followed in behind, shoving gently until we were both into a larger expanse of water. Without looking too closely, I knew we had landed in the fourth chamber and both of us seemed to be in good shape. Importantly, our cylinders still contained more than enough gas to get us home. I popped my head briefly above the water and then submerged once more, feeling my way forward in the dark, trying not to pull on the rope for fear of dislodging it, all the while keeping a careful eye out for the left turn that would signify the home stretch towards dive base. Once past it, the surface would be only 50 metres away.

Really, the hardest work had been done. As long as the bubbles drifting up from Tern's mask remained steady, he would probably survive what had been a harsh ordeal. Though he had been an unknowing passenger, the poor boy had probably taken one or two bumps and scrapes to his arms and legs. Meanwhile, I was bloody knackered – physically and emotionally. My muscles ached; my brain wanted to drift away into a long and restful sleep, and my ears and sinuses throbbed from yet another building infection. What had started as a head cold was now a pounding face-ache, another consequence of ten days spent working in filthy water. I had survived so far on decongestants and a snort of nasal spray every couple of hours. It wasn't ideal; I would very much suffer in the coming days, but there was no way I was bailing out on the rescue mission now.

The junction came and went, the floor of the cave rose up to meet us and I could feel the mud and pebbles beneath me as I dragged Tern forward. *Chamber three and dive base weren't too far away. From there the military would whisk him away for medical treatment.* And then, unexpectedly, my passenger felt incredibly heavy. He wouldn't move. I pulled gently on the strap attached to his back in an attempt to edge him towards safety, careful not to compromise his mask, but he remained steadfast. Tern was bloody stuck. *And now of all places!* I tried again, yanking harder this time, but whatever was holding the boy in place had grabbed him tight. I felt edgy once more. Though our cylinders were over half full, a lengthy process of digging or untangling someone in such a vulnerable and exposed position as Tern might take some time, especially if I was to avoid injuring him. The comfort zone of air in both our tanks would diminish very quickly.

I looked down. It was impossible to see past Tern's shoulders in the swirling, brown waters, so there was no option other than to park him at the bottom of the chamber, but that was a delicate process. Taking care that the cylinder affixed to his chest would stop his face and regulator from plunging into the mud and rock below, I unclipped the passenger from my body and secured him to the line. Now able to move freely, I patted him down like a nightclub bouncer, until I located the cause of his problem: a length of old black telephone wire had wrapped around his right calf and was lassoing him to the spot. Thankfully, the lines were decommissioned, so I wouldn't have to manage them with too much caution. Instead, I made two cuts with my shears, and slowly pulled Tern free, before carefully looping my arm over the guideline and reattaching him to my harness. The last thing I had wanted was to lose contact with our route to dive base, especially as we were less than five minutes away. The hum of water pumps was growing louder. Our journey was done.

My head broke the surface. The lights of chamber three felt glaring, and I was struck by the intense activity moving around us. Even before I had surfaced, my spasmodic jerks on the line as it broke surface had been noticed. I heard shouting and the announcement that a diver had returned safely. *Fish on!* Several pairs of hand reached down to pull the boy from the water. And then a well-practised chain of events fell into place in which Tern was hauled free, hoisted on to a stretcher and checked over before being dragged away by ropes. I barely had time to unclip. If I hadn't, there's every chance I'd have been dragged along with him, such was the urgency in getting him to treatment.

One of the US Air Force rescue team leant down to help.

'Is he alive?' I asked.

He nodded. *Yes.*

Relieved, I collapsed back into the water, dragged down by the weight of my gas cylinders. I had done all I could for the boy. The diving was finished. We had negotiated all the flooded sections. Now he was out of my hands as he started his journey through the dry parts of the cave.

I was emotionally spent and utterly exhausted. My mind was under siege, too. As I watched Tern's body disappear around the corner, the intense loneliness that had struck me inside chamber nine returned. Only twelve divers had been allowed into the cave beyond chamber three, to simplify what was still a dangerous rescue plan. An army of military personnel, medical staff, and volunteers were now working between the dive base and the entrance and were moving the child on; all of them focused on Tern's wellbeing, and rightly so. Still, it was hard not to feel invisible. I sat in the water and gathered myself together. *Was I really expected to make the same trip tomorrow? And the next day?* The thought of it was bruising. But stepping down wasn't an option.

I looked around for support. Jason, ever the consummate professional, was nowhere in sight: having safely delivered his boy, he had decided to begin his preparations for another intense rescue dive the following day. That was how he worked, and I respected it. But Chris and Rick were due to appear at any moment, that's if everything had gone to plan. They would need some help when getting out of the water; their cylinders would take some dragging up the bank. I really didn't want them to experience the same heavy mood of abandonment that had overwhelmed me, especially if tragedy struck either of their passengers. It was one thing to feel alone having successfully rescued a boy. Rising up in the water with a corpse could prove psychologically devastating.

One by one, the divers appeared, their imminent arrival signalled by a gurgle of bubbles in the sump and the twitching of the line. Their shadows seemed to ripple; it was possible to spot the masks and air cylinders as two figures sharpened into focus beneath the surface – rescuer and rescued. Chris arrived first, looking drained. The trip had taken its toll. Rick showed up soon after, acting as if it had been just another routine exploration. Then our support divers came in, until eventually, Harry's head popped above the water.

'How did we do?' he shouted anxiously.

Four for four!

His face dropped. Harry looked broken. 'Fuck, mate . . . *We killed them all?*'

No, they all survived!

Harry smiled. The look of relief was telling. Nobody could quite believe we'd gone and bloody done it.

Having relived this episode over and over, there is little doubt in my mind that the mission would have been scrapped, had one of the boys been killed that day. Thankfully, everyone had come through, and so the authorities were happy for us to proceed. We stripped out of our wetsuits and checked over the masks and equipment in preparation for our next dive the following morning. Unbelievably, the air reserves that had been staged throughout the cave were barely dented. With support divers due to take in replacements, there would be sufficient resources for the next forty-eight hours and our work could be repeated without a huge resupplying effort. Our only concern now was how to keep the next four boys alive. But to do so, we would have to make a habit of our opening day's success.

THE GAMIFICATION OF SUCCESS

One way of driving habitual success is to use the travelator theory, as discussed in Lesson #1, by first taking the simplest steps towards whatever end goal we're striving for, *but with diligence.* This might be the downloading of the correct application letter for a business grant, or a phone call to the estate agents in the exact area we want to move to. These actions might feel like tiny steps in an otherwise huge commitment; however by stepping aboard the travelator with extreme care, and therefore breaking down the challenge into significantly smaller and manageable chunks, we need only complete the next seemingly tiny task to advance. And the next. *And the next.* Before we know it, serious progress has been made.

Sometimes a commitment can take its toll, though. The process becomes boring; the travelator feels slow – it might even grind to a halt. One painstaking and time-consuming activity I engage in before every dive is the preparing of each and every aspect of my equipment with an exceptionally high level of diligence. Although it's a relatively easy process, it is also one with a large number of steps, and it would be very easy to skip some, or to cut corners. But that's a risk I'm not prepared to take. While I have often made jokes about wanting a 'caving butler', someone on hand to prepare my equipment for me, the truth is I would be unwilling to delegate these tasks. Cave exploration has taught me that no matter how experienced a diver is, if they haven't looked after their kit correctly, it's unlikely to look after *them* inside the cave. Taking these steps is my key to success and I repeat them habitually.

A more relatable example for most of us might be the introduction of a new nutrition plan, a commitment that can sometimes feel almost impossible during the early phases. After all, who really wants to embark on six weeks of reduced carbs and minimal sugar? But if a dieter prepares their meal plans and batch cooks in advance with diligence, they'll find the overall challenge easier to manage.

Of course, executing procedures of this kind are easier said than done, which is where the concept of *gamification* comes in to play. I first heard the term in 2008, and it has since come to signify the idea of bringing fun or rewarding elements into an otherwise mundane or difficult event, examples of which include education, rehabilitation, work productivity, exercise, responsible spending and that tricky nutrition plan. The key to gamification's success centres upon dopamine: the neurotransmitter that stimulates our brain's pleasure receptors whenever we achieve, and as a result incentivises us to concentrate, feel motivated and learn. It's the reason why so many of us get a mini 'high' after reaching a target or surpassing a previous best.

By gamifying ordinary but important tasks, we can make them habitual. For example, the idea of *a winning streak* and the satisfaction in maintaining it is a facet of many computer games – it can be incredibly rewarding having maintained an impressive run of victories on *Fortnite* or the FIFA football game. But I have found that by applying the same concept to activities such as running, I am able to stick to my targets and long-term goals more easily. If my training schedule demands a certain weekly mileage, I'll keep track of my work and take great satisfaction when maintaining the programme over a series of weeks and months. The idea, though, is for the process to be fun and quietly rewarding, rather than a stick to beat myself with. The same concepts can be applied to building fitness or giving up smoking or drinking. (*Ever heard of Dry January?*) Anyone in need of assistance will find there are a host of apps that can chart our progress in whatever challenge we've embarked upon.

In Tham Luang, the work was gruelling, and the challenges were severe. Every single diver working in the caves had been exhausted by the events of the first day and it was a slog to keep going. But there was no other choice but to press ahead until the Wild Boars were safely out. I used the concept of a winning streak to maintain forward momentum throughout the extractions. *One day down, one boy rescued. Two days down, two boys rescued* . . . In much the same way that a primary school teacher might use a star chart to motivate younger pupils, so I was tracking the successes.

My style of gamification was undeniably darker, though. Rather than planning a massive celebration or attempting to draw some form of joy or satisfaction when swimming Tern to safety, I simply focused on the elements of Lesson #5. Step one: take three seconds and breathe. Step two: take three minutes and think about keeping the boy alive. Step three: take three hours and get back to dive base in one piece. All those things combined acted as a powerful motivator. My success so far had been a result of good habits – patience, commitment and due diligence. Careful preparation underpinned my confidence and propelled me forward.

MAKE SUCCESS A HABIT: THE CHECKLIST

- Gamify chores. Count winning streaks.
- Complete tasks. Don't skip the small ones.
- Create structure. Build routine.

LESSON #13

DEFINE YOUR OWN HAPPINESS

What is success? In the context of the Tham Luang operation it was the extraction of all twelve Wild Boars and their coach over three days without serious injury. This was a team effort in which I am proud to have played my part. I wanted to say, 'I did OK'. There was no need to set records, or to save all thirteen people singlehandedly. Instead I set a satisfactory target and despite some undeniable road bumps along the way, I worked steadily towards it. However, it's possible for all of us to do something similar no matter the challenge ahead because we are the gatekeepers for our benchmarks and feelings. By managing them carefully, we're able to create our own happiness levels . . .

DAY FOURTEEN
MONDAY 9 JULY 2018
- - - - - - - - - - - - - - - - - -

Adul was out cold. He had first stirred before chamber five and having dragged him out of the water, I stuck a ketamine-loaded syringe into his thigh, just as Harry had done an hour or so previously. The needle slipped easily through his wetsuit and I could only hope that the dose had been measured accurately. My early first-aid lessons and those smiley orange faces had done nothing to prepare me for a moment such as this. Meanwhile, Harry's reassuring words that I would inevitably 'shit myself' in such a situation, only hinted at the fear I was now experiencing. I felt cold and isolated. The chamber was silent, apart from the occasional ripple and drip of water pooling about me somewhere.

A sudden noise caused me to look up. I was hyper-alert and on edge, which was unsurprising given that I'd been hunched over an unconscious boy with a syringe in my hand – I must have looked like the perpetrator of some terrible murder. As my vision adjusted to the shadows, Josh Bratchley, a British support team diver, materialised in front of me. He had been waiting for my arrival so we could move Adul into the next sump together.

'How is he?' he said, leaning down check on the boy's wellbeing. 'It's OK, Adul. It's going to be OK . . .'

The jury was still out on that one. Adul was a lot bigger than Tern. Having moved him away from the ninth cavern, where now only six boys and coach Ek – plus the Navy SEALs – had been left to wave us off cheerily, I had been struck by the boy's size; I even worried that he might prove too big for the journey. *Would I be able to squeeze the kid through the narrow gap between chambers five and four without injuring him?* But there was no time to ponder. In the end I had adjusted to my new cargo fairly quickly, cradling Adul's head under my chin and pulling him along in much the same way as I had done with Tern. We'd soon found a steady pace. Checking on the boy's condition had been a hell of a lot easier, too: Adul breathed like a steam train. Plumes of bubbles exploded around me with every exhalation. The report card from the halfway mark read: *so far, so good.*

'Yes, he's fine . . . I think,' I said.

But I had spoken too quickly. Having readied Adul for the next leg of the journey, we replaced his face mask, but something felt off. When I looked down to check, the boy had stopped breathing.

Shit! *Was he dead?* I removed the mask and ran through the same procedures as yesterday, tilting his head back, listening in close, hoping to hear or feel some faint gasp or a sign that his lungs were still functioning. But there was nothing. My heart sank. *Had I overdosed him?* I looked up at Josh in alarm. The nightmare moment had arrived, and I used my psychological rehearsals to adopt a rational approach to what was becoming a very panicked situation.

When a person falls unconscious, their hearing is the final sense to fade. That's why nurses and emergency services workers reassure their casualties with gentle words of comfort – the stricken individual might still be able to hear. Josh, in his politest voice, attempted to coax the boy back to life.

'Come on, Adul. You can do this. Breathe. *Breathe . . .*'